Orkney
All the Way Through

To the memory of my father

Orkney
All the Way Through

GEORGE GARSON

JOHN DONALD PUBLISHERS LTD
EDINBURGH

ISBN 0 85976 362 5

British Library Cataloguing in Publication Data
A catalogue record for this book is available from the British Library.

Typeset by the Midlands Book Typesetting Company, Loughborough
Printed in Great Britain by Arrowsmith Ltd., Bristol

Acknowledgements

Blessings, J. Gunn, for your book *Orkney the Magnetic North*, which gave me so much pleasure that war-girt summer of 1941. My indebtedness also, to the writings of Ernest W. Marwick, Edwin Muir, George Mackay Brown, John Firth, Hugh Marwick, Liv Kjörsvik Schei, John W. Hedges, Patrick Bailey, and the totally readable and unpompous face of Scotland's National Monuments, Anna Ritchie.

1992   George Garson

Contents

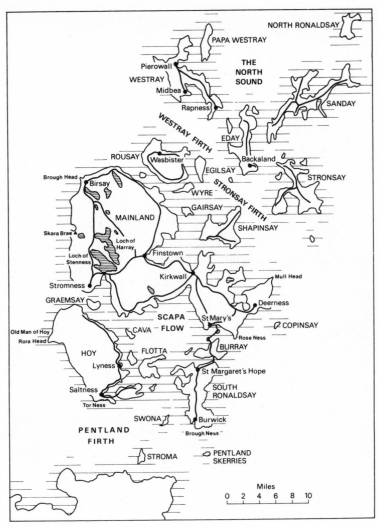

NORTH RONALDSAY

PAPA WESTRAY

THE
NORTH
SOUND

Pierowall

WESTRAY

Midbea

Rapness

SANDAY

WESTRAY FIRTH

EDAY

Backaland

ROUSAY

Wasbister

EGILSAY

STRONSAY

Brough Head

Birsay

WYRE

STRONSAY FIRTH

MAINLAND

GAIRSAY

Skara Brae

Loch of
Harray

SHAPINSAY

Loch of
Stenness

Finstown

Stromness

Kirkwall

Mull Head

GRAEMSAY

Deerness

SCAPA

St Mary's

COPINSAY

CAVA

FLOW

Rose Ness

Old Man of Hoy

BURRAY

Rora Head

HOY

FLOTTA

Lyness

St Margaret's Hope

Saltness

SOUTH
RONALDSAY

Tor Ness

SWONA

Burwick

PENTLAND

Brough Ness

FIRTH

STROMA

PENTLAND
SKERRIES

Miles

0 2 4 6 8 10

Location Map

Introduction

'You'll chust huf got back from the Isles then, Chorge,' the man at the bar said, in that embarrassing impersonation some Lowland Scots equate with people and things Highland and Island. 'What's that Gaelic toast for "good health", again?' 'Slan-ji Va!' his friend replied, bending his elbow.

I'd heard it all before, of course. And, depending on my mood, either blow up or shut up and sup up.

As much as I enjoy the gnarled horizons, peaks, moorlands, and that sense of yearning which, for me, is North West Scotland (for there's Tiree blood in me, too), it isn't Orkney. Orcadians for one thing don't, as they say, 'have the Gaelic', but speak with Nordic cadences. The majority of the islands (with one notable exception) are sweetly curved, cultivated and green. And, contrary to popular belief, are a ferrie's distance north of Thurso, *not* hemmed-in by a box somewhere in the North Sea, 150 miles east of Aberdeen. And yes, there are gales. And winters with a handful of hours of grudged daylight. Though nothing that a sardonic sense of humour, a tight roof, TV and a good-drawing coal fire won't ease.

The Orkney Islands (70 in all) are made up in the main of sedimentary rocks. Unlike the sterner Scottish granites, it splits sweetly into manageable slabs of an even thickness, and must have come as a godsend to the early settlers. I'm saddened by its gradual demise architecturally for the ubiquitous and wholly inappropriate kit-built bungalow, complementing as it did, the horizontal nature of the land, and the abiding presence of the sea. Author and naturalist, Jim Crumley, says it all in his poem, 'Orkney all the way through':

> Orkney rock is stacked
> and stashed away like fishboxes
> disassembled only
> by the fingering, punching sea.

1

Split and hewn it makes
staunch and stubborn dykes
sea-wall benches
and wind-wise gables

or stands obediently
in tombstone wafers; sometimes
it takes on a life of its own
and gathers in unearthly parliaments

at Brodgar or Stenness
debating eternity's laws.
Cut it and it letters 'Orkney'
all the way through.

That Orkney's climate — that kaleidoscope of weather moods — gets a bad press, is true. As I've said, there are gales, some legendary. Like the one in 1952 which caused my friend, Davo Craigie's henny hooses to become airborne, and were last seen — and heard — heading for the Pentland Firth. There's rain, too, due to low pressure in the Atlantic. And summers are rarely unbearably hot. But winters, thanks to the Gulf Stream, are mild, and snow is powdery and rarely lies for any length of time. And I've known dry and sun-bright Februarys, when skies were Swiss-blue and cloudless; the air scouring the lungs. Whilst southern cities were reduced to impotent snarls, wheel-deep in curses and slush.

Trees, as we know them in Lowland Scotland, are few. There are no plumed poplars, pines, or conker-laden horse chestnuts to mar the wind-cuffed horizons. But bog cotton and heather sweeten the moors. There are rare alpines and wild orchids, and wall-to-wall carpets of thrift, buttercups, marsh marigolds, wild lupins and daffodils. Here, too, are lepidoptera with melifluent Latin names: *Maniola jurtina, Thera juniperata, Aprophyla lutelanta lueneburgensis.*

For many, Orkney's great attraction is its vast colonies of sea birds. The Atlantic facing cliffs of Hoy and Mainland, and the bird reserves on some of the North Isles are a must for bird nuts, and teem with raucous rabbles of gulls, kitiwakes, terns, guillemots, and that insouciant thermal dawdler, the fulmar.

2

Call some native-born Orcadians 'Scottish', at your peril. For there are many, still, who, despite the considerable Scottish admixture, regard themselves as descendants of those Norsemen who colonized Orkney around AD 800. That there is no trace of a Scots accent will come as a surprise to first-time visitors. An Orcadian's speech is rhythmic with a rising cadence and emphasis on the last syllable. I've heard similar speech rhythms from hard-drinking knots of Norwegian trawlermen in harbour bars. Although some of the old Norse words — the Okrney Norn — linger, many of the splendid words commonly used by my crofting relatives have given way to tabloid-speak and the banal mouthings of TV soap stars. Rarely, if ever, do we hear such grand old words as *clagum*, for toffee. Or *clep*, for a handful of mud. *Dolimentin*, scintillating, or shining. And the lovely *leesom*, for the coming of the night.

The good news is that unemployment fell from 12.6 per cent in 1986 to 7.6 per cent in 1990. Small industries and quality craft workshops thrive. Fat beasts chomp succulent grass in immaculate fields. Boats stacked with creels putter out of harbours. And local shops — so far — are free from the 'Viking' equivalent of the obscene tourist tartanalia which scabs our dourly dignified Scottish towns and cities.

Orcadians are welcoming and kindly, speak in direct, no-nonsense tongues; are dry of wit, ambitious, well-informed, hard-working. They are more than tolerant of those incomers humble and wise enough to honour and respect their traditions and indigenous ways. This book is an unashamedly subjective celebration of those people, and of the place I call home.

CHAPTER ONE

Stromness

There's a spume-flecked yarn hereaboots, of how, during a particularly vicious Pentland Firth crossing on board *St. Ola* (I) a North Company VIP sharing the skipper's pitching bridge asked tremulously where the nearest land might be. To which the master, pointing at the deck beneath the VIP's gaitered boots, with typical Orcadian wit replied, 'Doon!'

She was black, blunt-stemmed, narrow-gutted, coal-fired and reeked of stale vomit and fear-filled cattle. But I know old Stromnessians who boast still of her legendary sea worthiness; and of how, with cocky panache, she plied continuously that fickle stretch of water from 1892 to 1951.

I feared and hated her!

Aficionados insist that the present one hour and forty minutes *St. Ola* (III) Scrabster to Stromness ferry-crossing is the most exciting approach to the Islands. In terms of cliff drama and human comforts alone, I'd agree. For, slab-sided and lumpish though she is, *St. Ola* (III) is a most reassuring and seaworthy P&O, roll-on-roll-off job, as different from her predecessors as a Viking longship is to a hollowed-out log.

There's a small, but well-stocked bar with medicinal nips for the squeamish; hot pies, bacon rolls and bridies for the truly heroic; tea or coffee for the green of gill; gaming machines and a lounge with soft couches to lay a child's head on.

Uptop, the Anorak'd Ones, cameras primed, gather on the starboard deck; for soon, two miles south of St John's Head (that slab-faced landlord to a rabble of fish gluttons), the best-known, most photographed rock stack in the world will reveal its aquiline snout behind the buttress of Rora Head.

The Old Man of Hoy (first climbed in 1966) is 450 feet high: its title evident if caught in near profile. Its considerable distance from shoreline and parent cliff is indicative of its great antiquity. And vulnerable though he may look, as white seas bark at his ankles, his feet, unlike his red sandstone head, consist of hard volcanic rock; of which J. Gunn in his book, *Orkney the Magnetic North*, touchingly writes:

> It is possible that the Old Man will never fall but that his end will come through the peaceful decay of old age, as that sandstone is slowly disintegrated by atmospheric weathering. Those who love the Old Man may find some comfort here.

From here on the coastline assumes Wagnerian proportions, rivalling those of St Kilda. Seabirds loiter on quixotic thermals; dive, wheel, zap; skite across endless seas and heckle for toeholds on the 1,000-foot-high crimson cliffs of St John's Head.

As the cliff drama falls astern, human-scaled ones begin: deckhands stand by mooring cables fore and aft. The seasick smile wanly. The young heave backpacks from lockers, and the Anorak'd Ones, eager for that first glimpse of Stromness, shift to the port side as the ferry skirts Hoy Sound's sly tidal flat spots (known to fishermen as 'blankets'), makes a deft port-hander round the Point of Ness, and, with practised dexterity, eases her visored snout into harbour.

First impressions are that this is no Scottish township: for Stromness, cooried in to the south-west corner of the Mainland, wears a gaithered th'gither Nordic look. A frieze of slate and stone-clad dwellings, piers, vennels and nousts, stitch the shoreline beneath Brinkie's Brae. Shags bask in the fitful sun. A seal fixes the folks fae Soothaboots with seen-it-all-before eyes. And lobster boats, decks laden with creels and floats, putter towards their hunting grounds.

Contrary to appearances, Stromness is younger than it looks. Smaller and less ancient than the capital town, Kirkwall, its history is a comparatively short one.

Sheltered as it is from westerly gales, it is obvious why this most natural of harbours was esteemed by Nordic longshipmen (as the old name Hamnavoe, 'haven bay', suggests) and eight-eenth-century whaler alike. There were, and still are, those who regret the demise of the Norse name: some who regarded the name Stromness as something of a misnomer, among which the Orcadian writer Hugh Marwick was one:

... one regrets that it was not named Hamnavoe. The name of the surrounding parish, however, was applied instead, and a certain ambiguity now sometimes arises through the use of the same name for both. That name — Stromness, 'tide-ness' — was originally applied to the ness or headland projecting into the swiftly racing Hoy Sound.

Then, warming to his dissertation, he continues:

... and for the guidance of strangers who somehow tend to mispronounce the name (and are copied by not a few simple-minded Orcadians trying to 'speak proper'), it may be well to point out that the accent falls on the first syllable, and not on the -ness.

Little is known about the town's earliest days, though it is likely that those attracted to the bay would have chosen to settle on the gently sloping Cairston shore, east of Brinkie's Brae. Records show that there was a house at Garson above the Bay of Navershaw at the end of the fifteenth century. The *Orkneyinga Saga*, too, relates how, on the morning of Michaelmas Day, Earl Harald Maddason and his men saw a longship coming towards them and, expecting trouble, ran from their own ships and took refuge in the Castle of Cairston (Kjarreksstaoir).

In 1642 feus were granted by the Bishop of Orkney for five houses (probably no more than thatched buts and bens) to be built on the west side of the harbour, on what is now Stromness. That the importance of the sheltered bay influenced this decision is obvious. Level building sites, though, must have been gey scarce; but by excavating the brae side and building up on the lower side, the problem could be solved. Moreover, with a little extra effort, why not extend the concept: have your very own pier, or state-of-the-art boatslip?

Although none of those earlier dwellings remain, it is tempting to imagine that the layout didn't differ all that much from Stromness as we know it. For here, unlike mainland Scotland, where planners are no more than renegade used-car salesmen, and mock-Georgian 'executive housing' scabs the face of the land, form and content are governed by the nature of the elements and indigenous common sense. Windows were, and still are, small and deeply set into thick stone walls. Surfaces, too, would have been rendered with that splendidly dour wet dash harling, so common once throughout Scotland.

And so the village grew according to the needs of the people. Unplanned. Gable ends jutting seawards.

In 1745 the population had risen to 600 when Alexander Graham, 'a native of this town,' made his 'little fight for freedom' against the Royal Burgh of Kirkwall. A disused and forlorn silver-painted drinking fountain, erected in 1901 at the pier head, says it all:

ALEXANDER GRAHAM
DIED 16th APRIL 1783
THIS FOUNTAIN IS ERECTED TO PERPETUATE
THE MEMORY OF ALEXANDER GRAHAM
A NATIVE OF THIS TOWN, WHO DURING THE
YEARS 1743 – 1758, AT GREAT PECUNIARY
SACRIFICE TO HIMSELF, FOUGHT THE
ROYAL BURGH OF KIRKWALL AS REPRE -
SENTING THE CONVENTION OF ROYAL BURGHS
IN THE LAW COURTS, AND WAS ULTIMATELY
SUCCESSFUL IN OBTAINING A VERDICT WHICH
FREED STROMNESS FROM PAYING CESS TO
KIRKWALL, AND AT THE SAME TIME, ALL OF THE
TOWNS IN SCOTLAND SIMILARLY SITUATED WERE
THUS DELIVERED FROM THE THRALLTY
OF THE ROYAL BURGHS

1901
ANDREW WYLIE
PROVOST

from then on, Stromness, like Topsy, just growed, its prosperity based on shipping and the wars in which Britain was involved between 1688 and 1815.

By the end of the eighteenth century the town's population was over 1,300, of which the ratio of males to females was no fewer than 21 to 12. It was no wonder then, that, local lads left in droves to work elsewhere. Some went to the American colonies and the West Indies. Others found employment in the 'Nor-Wast' with the Hudson's Bay Company and whaling. Orcadians, it is said, comprised three-quarters of the Company's Canadian workforce. Ships large and small lay at anchor in harbour and roadstead, and over 800 are said to have called in a year.

Skullduggery ruled, too: and none more skullduggered than the Orkney pirate, John Gow (1698–1725), the 'Cleveland' of Walter Scott's forgettable novel *The Pirate*. Gow was born in Caithness and settled in Stromness with his father, William Gow, merchant, around 1710. Educated in Stromness, he became a deep-sea sailor, and shortly thereafter embarked on his brief (approximately eight months) career as a pirate, after being elected skipper by the mutinous crew of the good ship *Caroline*, which he subsequently, and most appositely, renamed *Revenge*.

Why he returned to his native Orkney when armed vessels were tailing his wake, no one knows. But while beating up Calf Sound he ran aground on the Calf of Eday, was captured, tried and hanged in London in 1725.

For me, though, it is the nineteenth century which truly haunts the straggle of vennels and squares with the spirit of place. By 1821 Stromness had a population of 2,944 in 385 houses. The main street was unpaved, glaury, and not at all to the liking of Sir Walter Scott who, when visiting Stromness in 1814, had said:

> The town cannot be traversed by a cart or even a horse, for there are stairs up and down even in the principal street ... whose twistings are often caused by a little inclosure before the house, a sort of yard, about twenty square feet called a park.

The village became a Burgh of Barony two years after the literary ferrylouper's visit. Trades and professions boomed; rates were levied (so what's new?); the streets were clad with slabs of Orkney stone, named, and lit by oil lamps.

Pubs, inns, schools, banks, a parish church, a post office and town hall bore witness to the Burgh's burgeoning prosperity. Boatyards dirled to the sounds of caulking mallet and ripsaw. Fleets of brightly painted 'Fifies' and 'Zulus' from the Moray coast, lug sails stained a deep red brown, unloaded their catches at harbour and quay. Stromness-owned schooners traded to Leith and Wick, Newcastle and Liverpool, with anything from cowhides to stockings. Here, too, the steamer *Royal Mail* was built and operated by John Stanger, a local shipbuilder, which served from 1856 to 1868, a service made possible by the newly built Scrabster pier.

The summer herring boom continued up to the end of the nineteenth century. Peripatetic female gutters and packers lived in local digs and in communal timber huts at the North and South ends. A kippering house fanned its reek across the barley stooks at Cairston Road. This influx of some 2,000 ancillary workers, in a town of less than 2,000 souls, put pressure — literally — on freshwater supplies and sewage disposal. Public and private wells were polluted, and the place stank to Valhalla.

Stromness continued to thrive up to the end of that war they call 'Great'. The depression years of the twenties and thirties however, saw a brave but short-lived revival of the herring industry and other marine-based ventures, as well as the closure of Stanger's boatyard.

The harbour is quieter now. Old men sit on painted benches: reminisce, coax pipes of dark tobacco, study their burnished toecaps. Boys fish with handlines from pier ends, their catches tarnishing in the sun. Tourists wind on metres of celluloid cliché and chatter in loud tongues. A dissonance of gulls forage among the floats and lobster creels, next to *Excelsior*, *Mara*, *Radiant Queen*, *Sharon Rose* and *Siobhan*, who rest level-keeled between harsh fishing stints, their decks hosed clean of fishscale, gut and broken claw.

The herring industry — though a mere whiff of its former self — is alive, well and flourishing in a former North End slaughterhouse. It is a small stone building, the exterior of which is virtually unchanged since I — a lad of ten — peered with compelling revulsion through its flyblown window, as men killed pigs with knives; hooves dinging convulsively on the concrete floor; blood sputtering on red rubber apron and wall.

The aprons are white these days, the interior clean, metallic and bright. Disenchanted with his former career, ex deep-sea master mariner, Ken Sutherland, came ashore for good, some years back, to launch and skipper *Orkney Marinated Herring* with a crew of four. It was an apt career switch for someone whose great great grandfather began the herring industry on the Isle of Stronsay. A rash of distribution points on a map of Britain on the office wall is evidence of his success.

Because of the short British herring fishing season (September to November), and cost, his raw material is shipped from Denmark in 90-kilo barrels packed with 1,500 fillets.

'Good quality stuff, eh?' he says, skinning a fillet with his thumb, to reveal the succulent dark flesh.

He is less forthcoming about the secret ingredients of exotic spices which give his tubs of plain, dill, and sherry marinated herring their unique flavour.

'Ah well, *that's* another story,' he said guardedly, as I shook his brine-pickled fist.

North End Road — unlike the sea-girt vistas of South End — is a neither yin-thing-nor-anither place. A huddle of wee garages, petrol points, an open air fruit and vegetable stall, and landlocked motor boats, kept at bay by the conservation area boundary of John Street.

But I like it for all that. For here, in dark lockups, their benches a Passchendaele of used filters and gaskets, men in grubby boilersuits will sweeten a sour engine with oaths and soft incantations.

I like to begin my north-to-south perambulation of this 1,000-metre dogleg of delights and architectural surprises at Speddings, a chemist of that name who lived here at John Street. For this is nineteenth-century Orkney vernacular at its finest: no folderals, no exterior conceits or confectionery.

The Miller's house, is tucked up a tight close. Named after the merchant family, Miller, and occupied continuously by their descendants since 1716, it is the earliest datable house in Stromness. Above the crimson door there's a fine armorial stone and the motto, 'God's Providence is my Inheritance'.

Drop anchor at nearby Ferry Inn for an excellent bar meal, or a snifter of whatever takes your fancy (I'll have a large Highland Park, thanks). Owned and superbly managed by Magnus and Maureen Dennison, this is a truly gregarious and international watering hole: a crowstepped haven for scallop fishermen, trawlermen, Scapa Flow wreck divers — male and female, pallid penpushers, and yachtpersons with close-hauled accents. (Thinks: 'It's hard to believe the Temperance Movement gained support and Stromness was declared "dry" by local referendum from 1920 to 1947.')

The building known as the Warehouse is eighteenth century, and houses the Tourist Office (*very* helpful folk, here), the P&O Ferry Office and the permanent exhibition, 'This Place Called Orkney'. All three fulfilling their functions to the letter during the months of July and August, when the narrow Stromness Streets, which were made for gull-mew and sea-sound, run deep with tourists and cars.

For this chiel, though, the town's unique character begins at the stone-flagged narrows of Victoria Street — give or take a pool room and a carry-out sweet-and-sour chicken or three. The post office wears a stalwart, pre-war, brass and mahogany look. Counterhands conduct their business with a smile, and speak with mellifluous tongues.

But it is the Pier Arts Centre — that uncut gem in the Orcadian crown — which will surprise those Soothlans who think the visual arts end points north of the Firth of Forth.

Formerly a coalstore and warehouse, the Centre was opened (not without some antagonism from the powers that be, I hear) in July 1979, to house a small, though comprehensive collection of paintings by the so-called St Ives School, gifted by Margaret Gardiner, Orkney lover and friend of Henry Moore, Ben Nicolson, Barbara Hepworth, and others of that ilk. Good though the collection is, the ever-changing kaleidoscope of sea, light, birds and boats glimpsed through the gallery window is a hard act to follow.

No mere showcase for that clutch of established semi-abstractionists, the Centre's policy of airing the works of local fledglings, Scottish up-and-comings, and such luminaries as Matisse, Herman, Bellany, thrived under the visionary and altruistic curatorship of Stromnessian, Erland Brown, who, threatened insidiously by those hydra-headed, late twentieth-century monsters, 'Cost Efficient' and 'Market Force', retired recently in order to paint full-time.

That Brown's successor should utilise the pier, proper, as a permanent sculpture court is obvious. For, as Barbara Hepworth's patinated bronze illustrates, there are two kinds of art: that which perishes when exposed to the elements, and that which thrives and grows in stature, the more the elements chuck at it.

From here on the street — as the Orcadian poet, George Mackay Brown, so enviably puts it — 'uncoils like a sailor's rope'. Narrow, rough-hewn streets give way suddenly to spacious areas of semi-classical pretensions; then close again with equally dramatic suddenness.

Lyness House is an architectural gem, flawed only by flawlessly modern roofing slates. Browse in the cosily cramped and civilised atmosphere of Stromness Bookshop, where you will find a wide selection of local and international titles. Venture through the Khyber Pass (yes, truly), and Puffer's Close, named after James Leask — nicknamed 'Puffer' — who was the town crier at the turn of the century. Explore Gray's Noust, too, and daunder up the demonically named, though wholly harmless, Hellihole Road.

It is Alfred Street, however, and No. 17 in particular, which quicken my memories, not only of a remarkable local woman, but also on an excitingly chaotic period in the town's history.

It was 1942. I was twelve years old. My father was a cook on a coastal rust bucket, her decks laden with corrugated iron and sullen boulders of tar. All manner of ships filled the harbour, and the streets were choked with mobile ack-ack guns, troop carriers, staff cars, close-ordered columns of morose squaddies, tiddly bow sailors, black marketeers and merchant seamen in baggy guernseys.

On the wind-scoured moors beyond Brinkie's Brae, anti-aircraft gunners, born within the sound of Bow Bells, yearned after a familiar bed, fourteen days' leave, a special woman's lips.

'The bloody Orkneys!' they called it. A place more foreign to a poor old conscript than the sands of Iwo Jima. A popular rhyme doing the rounds at that time sums it up. I've heard cruder and more apposite variations, but the following expurgated version attributed to one, Captain Hamish Blair, will do:

The bloody roads are bloody bad
The bloody folks are bloody mad
They make the brightest bloody sad
   in bloody Orkney

Best bloody place is bloody bed
With bloody ice on bloody head
You might as well be bloody dead
   in bloody Orkney.

The *St. Ola*, gun-mounted now and no longer permitted to sail through Scapa Flow, carried passengers and mail west-about to Scrabster via Hoy Sound, a route she was to ply with her sister ship, the dreaded *Earl of Zetland*, throughout the war.

A colleague, illustrator, writer and ex ack-ack soldier, John Mackay, remembers her well:

> The *Earl of Zetland?* Once sailed in, never to be forgotten! She was a small, top-heavy motor troop ship ... a dance hall now, or something, moored at Clacton, or some such place. One of my London mates told me of a gunner, going on leave; done up in his dress artillery uniform, wallowing in the sick in the scuppers, as she sailed for Scrabster. But worse was to come, after making it across the Pentland Firth, she couldn't make the harbour mouth at Scrabster, so had to do an about-turn back to Stromness!

It was against this backcloth that I first lived under No. 17 Alfred Street's benevolent roof.

Mrs Johnston — or 'Mrs J.', as everyone called her — was a small, sharp-eyed and vigorous white-haired legend in a crossover peeny, who kept open house to all and sundry, civvy and military, the Orcadian term of endearment, 'buddo, buddo', never far from her lips as she plonked steaming mounds of jacket potatoes and whole boiled hens, topped with Orkney butter, onto the scrubbed deal table.

It was she who, one sleet-blashed day in 1914, spied through her tiny gable-end ground-floor window with its uninterrupted view of the street a downcast, 14-year-old galley boy, invited him in, fed him from her ever-simmering black cooking pots, polished his boots and washed and ironed his shirt, as he warmed himself at the peat fire. It was to become an act of kindness my father repaid with love, throughout and beyond her long life.

Her ever-open door is shut, the rooms converted to dour striplit offices by the Orkney Fishermen's Society: processors of crabs and lobsters for destinations Soothaboots and Continental.

That Orcadian landladies are known for their hamespun courtesy goes without saying. Not, though, according to the following observation by English writer and traveller, J. Emerson, who, in 1652, wrote:

An Orkney wife to the life . . .
A cod's great head wrapt in a dirty clout,
An Owle's fairie eyes, Baboone's sweete face, Hound's eares,
Back of an able Mare (a jade that beares
Her burden well). The belly of a brindled cow,
Behemoth's legges, Bare's feet, an Apes arse and
A stinking shoulder of mutton for each hand:
These put together are the very same
Letters that spell my Landladye's right name,
. . . Find Belzebub and every deadly sin,
Thous't found my Landlady and all her kin.

No Tourist Board huckster, he.

Contrary to popular belief, Orcadian poet and writer, George Mackay Brown, does *not* live in some stone-flagged peat-reeking but and ben on the edge of a sea-cuffed cliff. No. 3 Mayburn Court is a cooncil hoose in a block of identical dwellings overlooking Stromness Museum, and a red pre-state-of-the-art phone box. The living room is small, welcoming and simply furnished: a favourite rocking chair, a couch for countless friends and fans, TV set and bookshelves.

Born in Orkney, he rarely travels beyond his native Stromness.

'I prefer to travel in me head,' is his firm, though typically courteous, reply to the obvious question.

Not only is he a princely poet, but also a renowned novelist, short-story writer, and teller of tales of Orkney life and history: of earls and kings, fishermen and crofters, whalers, tinkers and martyred saints. In short, the man's a genius.

He probably won't speak to me ever again.

Stromness Museum was founded in 1837 by the Orkney Natural History Society, and is everything a museum should be. Creaky underfoot and charmingly dingy, it is supervised (make that 'lovingly tended') by the far from creaky Jeannie Firth, who tells me she has never had a day off, or been late since taking up the post on 6 June 1962.

A chamber pot, a bosun's whistle, barnacle-encrusted mugs, a sailor's cap, ship's binnacle, bell and other relics from the German Fleet scuttled at Scapa Flow in 1919, have pride of place on the ground floor, along with whaling and other salty memorabilia, like the inlaid sea chest belonging to Captain John Smith of Cockleha', Tankerness, who was butchered by a mutinous crew on board his ship, *Flowery Land*, en route for Singapore.

Upstairs, in the natural history section, there are glass cases with strict rows of crustacea, mollusca, fossil fish, Stone Age arrowheads, beads, a comb, polished bone pins and nobly faded stuffed birds.

As I said, it is everything a museum should be. Though no doubt some committee, in its infinitesimal wisdom, will haul it into the twenty-first century, strip it, stuff it with audio-visual screens, fibreglass Vikings, and rename it Orkney Interpretation Centre.

Tak tent to Login's Well. Sealed up in 1931, the well supplied water to the ships of the Hudson's Bay Company: to Captain Cook's vessels *Resolution* and *Discovery* in 1780; and to Sir John Franklin's ships *Erebus* and *Terror* on Arctic expedition in 1845.

Southend, unlike Northend, which begins with a whimper, ends at Ness Road on an explosion of seascape and sky.

Weather permitting, I love to soak in the view from one of the six haemorrhoidal stone benches nearby. Or draw breath beside the American privateer's cannon.

The house and walled garden of Stenigar, formerly Stanger's boatyard, was converted shortly after the Second World War by the many lettered Orkney artist, Stanley Cursiter. (Observant visitors will have noticed the fine seascape of his in Stromness

Museum.) This is an excellent building, crafted from local stone, in complete harmony with the *genius loci*, and free from those fykie 'features' so beloved of today's developers.

The golf course, too, has its charms, they tell me. As does the caravan and camping site at the Skerry of Ness. Fine. But I'll settle for a daunder round the Point of Ness, and along the western shore, where oystercatchers ploiter at the Noust of Nethertown. And seas cream on Pulse Skerry, Kirk Rocks and the distant coast of Hoy.

CHAPTER TWO

West Mainland

As the name suggests, Mainland is the largest of Orkney's sixty islands, give or take a rock or two. Consisting of fourteen parishes it is divided into two unequal parts at the isthmus between Scapa Bay and the Bay of Kirkwall, and the strangulated strip of land at the parish of Deerness. The larger area to the west of Kirkwall is known as West Mainland, and the other, smaller area, as East Mainland.

The Bridge of Waithe — or Brig o' Waithe, as it is known — is approximately two miles from Stromness on the A965.

It was in this idyllic sea- and loch-fringed spot that 27-year-old labourer, James Isbister, on the night of 16 March, 1940, became the first civilian air-raid casualty of the war, as German planes jettisoned their bombs onto the clutch of cottages at the Brig.

I was cheered, though, to see signs of building work on the ruined cottage at the junction of the A965 and A964; formerly the howff and home of Willie Farquhar, garrulous dispenser of local gossip and stewed tea, in a room filled with peat reek and an assortment of burst, fourth-hand fireside chairs.

A cobbler to trade, Willie, like all Orcadians then, kept open door to all and sundry, and as the place's popularity grew he obtained a licence to sell tobacco, sweets and lemonade. Cobbling gave way to catering. Lonely soldiers, peat cutters, farmers, the crews of Continental cargo ships, and local folks travelling between Kirkwall and Stromness dropped in for a mug of tea and a hot pie.

As the premises became increasingly grimy and rundown, it was dubbed The Golden Slipper. Willie left Orkney in the late sixties and the howff stood empty and ruinous until it was bought some six years back. A three-bedroomed house, and a one-bedroomed 'granny' flat (how he would have laughed at that fatuous term) rise fitfully from the rubble.

Building blocks also rise between the scaffolding of the fire-gutted Standing Stones Hotel, formerly Orkney's most popular watering hole for plus-foured fishing types and their sensibly shod wives. We never dreamt of crossing its hallowed threshold when I was a lad, for this was where 'they' spent their endless summer vacations; the chattering classes, freed from bank and academia. Dressed in brogues, threadbare tweeds and raincoats no self-respecting working man would be seen alive in. 'Aye, boy, but it's funny what you can get away with when you've a wheen o' money,' my elders would say.

I did, however, drop in for a dram one sharp autumn noon some years back, and was saddened, though hardly surprised, to see the obligatory gaming machine blinking malevolently beneath a plaster cast sea trout in a scummy glass case. The lounge bar was empty and stank of sour beer. The service, sullen. One can only hope that S.S.H. mark (II) will manage to re-create something of its former charm.

Fishing on Orkney's six well-stocked lochs is free. But remember the common sense code: ask permission before entering private land. Take your spent lager tubes and such-like back to your car. Remember also that Orkney's many whooper and mute swans no more relish an apéritif of *Woodcock and Yellow* than you would.

The Stones of Stenness on the offside fringes of the B9055 date from the third millenium BC. Only four remain from a circle of twelve, the tallest of which is over fifteen feet high. Individually, I find them more awesome than those at the Ring of Brodgar. Look out also for two nearby standing stones, particularly the so-called Watch Stone, an imposing guardian of the narrow causeway.

John Thompson, bird carver, and his wife, Lesley Murdoch, ceramist, moved from the Borders in 1989 to their present home at Bridgend on the narrow isthmus close the the Ring of Brodgar. It's a humble corrugated iron dwelling, and a cramped masterpiece of form allied to function, with exhibition areas and a workshop you couldn't swing a red-throated diver in. Not that John Thompson would want to, for his is a respectful, almost mystical attitude towards the local waders, shags, herons and mergansers that inspire his art. 'I try to capture the species of the bird — its essence — just by watching and feeling, and by avoiding too much surface detail, though parallels to a birds plumage are created by using the direction of the wood's grain, and by controlled burning, staining, sanding and polishing.'

His raw materials — cypress and Scotch pine — come from such places as Golspie and Dunkeld, and are bought in such quantities — four to five tons at a time — as to last him for four years. Transportation costs, he said, are often beyond his means, then grins: 'The cattle people are good to me, though, and often bring some of it up in their trucks.'

Lesley, his wife, studied at Duncan of Jordanstone College of Art, Dundee, and graduated with a BA in ceramics in 1982. After working in Perth for two years, firing salt glazed porcelain in a wood-burning kiln, she moved to the Borders, and changed to an electric kiln and earthenware, to create hand-built planters decorated with coloured slips and bright glazes. Hers is a vivacious, bright, linear imagery, which focuses mainly on aspects of the human head and face, especially the eyes which, she claims, '... focus all emotion and mood.'

Their works are caringly and imaginatively crafted, modestly priced, sell well to those who know their arts from their elbow, and contradict the cynical, though all too true fact, that no one ever lost money by underestimating public taste.

Cliché, my *Collins English Dictionary* tells me, is 'a word or expression that has lost much of its force through over exposure'. I'd go further than that, and, by courtesy of tea towel, tourist tout and shortbread tin, add Edinburgh Castle, John Knox's House and the Scott Monument to that definition.

The Ring of Brodgar, give or take a desperately atmospheric colour postcard or three, disdainfully evades such Lowland toshery. Forebye, it's difficult, if not impossible, when photo-graphing this henge at ground level, to convey the drama of that immense circle. Aerial shots are much better, particularly those of freelance Swedish photographer, Gunnie Moberg, who has lived in Orkney since 1978.

The ring stands on a raised neck of moorland between the lochs of Stenness and Harray, surrounded by a broad ditch dug from solid bedrock. There are 27 stones in all, although reliable sources say there were originally 60 stones in the circle, which measures 103.7 metres in diameter.

It would be a moribund imagination, indeed, that remained unmoved by the atmosphere surrounding this third millenium BC ceremonial complex. Less well preserved than Stonehenge, I find it more gripping — due partly to its windswept location — than its imprisoned and much publicised sister. Stand in the centre of the circle beneath a pandemonium of stars, as I did one sharp winters night, and you'll see what I mean.

As to its original function no one knows for certain. Any one of the following uses seem plausible: lunar observatory; parliament; court of law; priesthood ceremonies for the burial of the dead; tribal rallying point. The sophistication of its structure, and the amount of labour required to raise the stones, are clues that it must have been a highly organised and skilled society.

Dr Robert Henry, the eighteenth-century antiquary, went further and christened the Ring of Brodgar the Temple of the Sun, and the Stones of Stenness, the Temple of the Moon. Rhapsodic though it sounds, it caught the mood of the times to such an extent that both locations became trysting places for young couples. Repairing (a nice archaism, that) first of all to the Temple of the Moon, the lass kneeled in front of her lover and prayed to the God Woden to honour and obey until death. After which both repaired to the Temple of the Sun, where the lad did likewise. The ceremony was concluded at the nearby Odin Stone (demolished in 1814) where an oath was made to Odin by clasping hands through the hole in the stone. A similar trysting stone known as Kipps Cromlech, can be found in the Bathgate Hills, West Lothian.

Orkney has many standing stones; more often single stumps in the centre of remote fields, many of which were, and perhaps still are, part of local folklore. The Orcadian temperament is the very antithesis of fey, but I've known farm folks who treated such objects within their boundaries with truculent respect.

Prior to, and shortly after the Second World War, before the voice of *Entrepreneurial Vulgaris* was heard in the land, Scotland's ancient monuments were places of pilgrimage. There were maps and books to devour on winter nights, in anticipation of that eagerly awaited seven days' summer holiday. And an imagination to gorge with unashamedly subjective historical fantasies.

We live in two-dimensional times, drip-fed on trivia. Incapable (or so it would seem to some chiefs of tourism) of forming our own opinions; dreaming *our* dreams; exploring the land and ancient stones of Scotland at *our* pace. Nudged discreetly, if need be, by sympathetic local guides. Conveyor-belt tourism is here to stay. Those things of which we are most proud have become archaeological consumer goods. What next? one wonders: an 'island experience' visitor attraction with trails, walkways and leaflets, round Kirkwall's Peerie Sea? A chip and putt golf course and conference centre on the Brough of Birsay? It's a problem closely monitored — often vehemently — by those who care for the continuance of Orkney's tenuously balanced way of life. And one which is aired regularly in *The Orcadian*; that fine newspaper which rightly assumes its readers can scan a page without moving their lips.

I read with disquiet bordering on depression that a certain tour operator forecasts a time when a fibreglass copy of Maeshowe may be needed. Due, I assume, to the gradual erosion by tourist breaths, of that monument's Viking graffiti.

Before the advent of interpretation centres and ticket booths, admission to many of Scotland's ancient monuments was by means of a key kept by the resident of some nearby cottage. It was a charming and couthy ritual. And I often recall that memorable day on which I first stood, short-trousered and scabby-kneed, in the heart of Maeshowe, the drama heightened by the greenish-yellow light from the hissing paraffin lamp, held aloft by the local custodian.

The tomb, apart from a few shards of skulls, was empty when James Farrer opened it in 1861. It was obvious it had been entered more than once. *Orkneyinga Saga* narrates how, during the struggle between the rival earls, Erland and Harald, for the control of the earldom:

> Earl Harald set out for Orkney at Christmas with four ships and a hundred men. He lay for two days off Graemsay, then put in at Hamna Voe on Mainland, and on the thirteenth day of Christmas they travelled on foot over to Firth. During a snowstorm they took shelter in Maeshowe [Orkahaugr] and there two of them went insane, which slowed them down badly, so that by the time they reached Firth it was night time.

The amazing skills of the Neolithic mason apart, it is the collection of runic inscriptions (the acceptable face of vandalism?) which gives Maeshowe its human stamp: 'Hermudr of the hard axe carved these runes'. 'Ingibjorg is the fairest of the women'. Other inscriptions by crusaders to the Holy Land record that 'Jerusalem-farers broke into Orkahaugr'. Here, too, are twig runes and other notable scratchings of serpent, walrus and dragon, drawn with typical Nordic panache. Other writings hint at treasure being borne '. . . out of this mound'.

That they were drunken mercenaries spurred by booze is more than likely. For no self-respecting native would dare disturb the mound dwellings of trows — those Scandinavian devils incarnate.

The village of Finstown was named after Irishman, David Phin, veteran of Waterloo and former landlord of The Toddy Hole, now The Pomona Inn. A bright and whimsical scatter of carved and painted folksy farmyard animals on a nearby bungalow wall, cause me, as usual, to overrun the unexpected left hander of the A966 to Aiker Ness and the Broch of Gurness in the parish of Evie.

A part-rutted, part-tarred car track skirts the Sands of Evie. I prefer to walk the sea's edge in the company of oystercatchers and turnstones. The Atlantic fretting at the mouth of Eynhallow Sound.

Brochs are sophisticated defensive hollow-walled structures, cooling tower in shape, and, in some cases, formed the nucleus of a settlement. They are a northern Scottish phenomenon, the best preserved and highest of which is the broch of Mousa, Shetland. Though stunted in comparison to its northerly neighbour, the Gurness broch (possibly first century BC) is worth a visit, if only to absorb its dramatically exposed location above the eroded ledge on the Point of Aikerness.

Its discovery in 1929 by the Orcadian poet, amateur conchologist and antiquarian, Robert Rendall, is the stuff that my boyhood dreams were made on. Whilst sketching on a knoll, a leg of his stool sank into the ground, and after shifting stones round about the hole, saw steps going into the mound.

He describes his discovery, thus:

> By sheer good luck the first thrust of the spade uncovered what proved to be the top opening of a narrow stone stairway set between solid walls. The inner wall, however, was of heavy flagstone, and by shining a torch between the chinks I could see that there were chambers of some kind behind it. A boy from the farm assisted me. As I progressed down step by step, he lowered a bucket on a rope so that I could fill it with the loose debris for him to draw up. I managed to clear about seven steps but, afraid of impending collapse of the inner wall upon me, I ceased from further excavation.

The road from the Broch of Gurness to the Brough of Birsay (both broch and brough have the same pronunciation as in loch not lock. Oil the epiglottis on Bach) is rich in offside sea views and evocative Nordic place and farm names: Spithersquoy, Nidgarth, Fisk Helia, Haafs Helia, Urigar. There's a close encounter with the Loch of Swannay, a zig and a zag between Swannay farm and Knowes of Lingro, a dogleg at Garthsetter, then a straight run towards Earls Palace, of which, more later.

What I've come to regard as the better part of me is due, partly, to those artists and writers who have reached into a place and touched its still centre. I think of Elgar and the Malverns; the Borders paintings of William Gillies; A. E. Housman's *Shropshire Lad*. The paintings of Paul Nash and Samuel Palmer. The American writers, Annie Dillard, Raymond Carver and Flannery O'Connor; all of whose works are rooted in reality, transfigured by vision. To this list I add the poetry and prose of Orcadian writer, George Mackay Brown. In particular, his novel, *Magnus*. I won't elaborate on this remarkable evocation of twelfth-century Orkney, steeped, as the blurb says in 'Norse legend, violent feuding ... and a sacramental form of martyrdom ...'. Borrow, or better still, buy it. Not only because it's a splendid read, but also for its relevance to the Brough of Birsay.

The Brough is a tiny uninhabited tidal island off the Point of Buckquoy, accessible (by foot only) by a strip of sea-ravaged concrete causeway and several yards of polished stones, scrunchy sand and rockpools. But Beware! Don't do as I did. Ensure that you know the state of the tide before crossing, as it rips in from the Atlantic at a fair old lick.

The man with the builder's barrow had no idea of the tides; said he was from Kirkwall, but that I 'should be allright'.

'Go for it! You'll have the island to yourself,' I thought, that tourist-free and cloudless February day. I did, too, the Kirkwall man's tepid assurance whispering at my ear as I picked my way between pool and stone, and the scrabbling and impatient sea.

There are few corners in my fairly wide wanderings in which, without conscious effort on my part, I have experienced a sense of place: that still centre I referred to earlier. The Brough of Birsay is one such place. Unadorned selfishness prevents me from revealing the location of the other. Whether due, in part, to the fact that I was alone in both instances, and that the sites were devoid of human chatter, I don't know.

Topographically, the Brough is a tilted plane which slopes gently from the causeway, and ends precipitiously on the puffin-encrusted cliffs, seawards. The remains of Celtic and Norse church settlements, plus the foundations of thirteen longhouses (communal dwellings) and a centrally heated hall and bath house, huddle in complex profusion on the grassy leeward slopes. But it is the shell of a tiny twelfth-century church, thirty strides long by three strides broad, which quickens the heart.

St Peter's Church, alias Peter Kirk, alias St Colms (after St Colm of Buchan and Caithness, not St Columba), alias Christ Church, is a surprisingly sophisticated building for its size, consisting of nave, choir and semi-circular apse. The altar dividing apse from choir is recently restored thirteenth-century. Reliable sources have it that the church's founder was

The Old Man of Hoy: Orkney's famous rockstack. Sketch by the author.

St Ola (1). Photograph, courtesy of the County Library, Kirkwall.

St Ola (111).

Old Stromness. Photograph, courtesy of the County Library,
Kirkwall.

The Golden Slipper, Stenness.

The Standing stones of Stenness.

John Thompson, wood carver, and his wife, Lesley Murdoch, ceramist, outside their cramped, though functional, corrugated iron-clad Bridgend studio close to the Ring of Brodgar.

Bird carvings by John Thompson.

Loch Stenness.

The Ring of Brodgar, Stenness. Sketch by the author.

Christ Church, Brough of Birsay.

Whale's vertebra, the shore of Birsay.

Stone dresser, Skara Brae Pictish Village.

Kelp drying. The ash from burned kelp was an important ingredient in the manufacture of iodine, glass and bleach, and was one of Orkney's main industries throughout the eighteenth and nineteenth centuries.

The Round Church, Orphir.

The Big Tree, Kirkwall.

ST. MAGNUS CATHEDRAL, FROM POST OFFICE LANE.

St Magnus Cathedral from Post Office Lane. The seventeenth
century spire in the photograph, was replaced in the early
twentieth century, by the green copper thrust we see today.
Photograph, courtesy of the County Library, Kirkwall.

Ola Gorrie; internationally renowned jeweller, and her mother, Minnie, at the entrance to the recently extended and highly sophisticated Kirkwall workshops. Photograph, courtesy of Charles Tait Photographic, St Ola, Orkney.

Pendant by Ola Gorrie.

Churchill Barrier.

Blockship off Churchill Barrier.

Raising of the battleship *Hindenburg*, Scapa Flow.

Robin Duncan says he has known "better times". In Burray parts, however, the name Duncan is still synonymous with quality boat building and repairs.

Lassies, garish with tassles, fringes and paper flowers, dress up as horses for The Festival of the Horse, St Margaret's Hope. Photograph, courtesy of Orkney Photographic, Kirkwall.

The traditional Easter ploughing match during The Festival of
the Horse, where boys compete with miniature ploughs on the
Sands o' Right. The lad who ploughs the straightest and neatest
furrow, wins. Photograph, courtesy of Orkney Photographic,
Kirkwall.

Betty Corrigall's Grave, Hoy.

The Dwarfie Stane, Hoy. Sketch by the author.

St Magnus Memorial, Egilsay.

St Magnus. Detail from a fifteenth century altarpiece; Andenes,
Nordland. Sketch by the author.

St Magnus Church, Egilsay.

Stone of Setter, Eday. Sketch by the author.

Traditional Orkney stone-slab roofing.

The island of Swona.

Earl Thorfinn, and that fifty years after his death it was raised to cathedral status.

A grave which some believe to have contained the martyred body of Magnus, prior to its interment in the cathedral, was discovered near the centre of the nave. Sceptics say it is more likely to have been that of the founder, Earl Thorfinn.

For me, George Mackay Brown gets closer to the truth in the following extract from the final chapter, 'Harvest', of his novel, *Magnus*:

> This man was now in two places at once. He was lying with a terrible wound in his face in the kirk where the old man and the old woman were girding themselves for the road: Birsay, place of his beginning and end, birth and sepulchre. Also he was pure essence in another intensity, a hoarder of the treasures of charity and prayer, a guardian.

A section of a Pictish symbol stone, found scattered over the graveyard, can be seen in the Royal Museum of Scotland, Edinburgh, the lower part of which is carved with three spear-bearing, bearded warriors ... the logo of the publishers of the book you read now. A convincing cast of this fine stone has been put up on site.

Skipi Geo is signposted at the causeway car park, and is a bonny coastal daunder between sea cliffs and fields of lush grass. This particular geo (a narrow opening in a cliff) forms a natural, sloping, stony beach harbour, and was used by fishermen since Viking times. A thatched nineteenth-century hut for storing equipment still stands. Traces of nousts (winter boat stores) can be detected in the adjoining strip of land. Each family was allocated one of these nousts, and shared the responsibility for its upkeep. By the nineteen sixties local fishermen used the area less and less, and the site fell into disrepair.

Beyond Birsay Bay is the 200 feet high mass of Marwick Head, on the summit of which stands a dour, four-square stone tower built in memory of Lord Kitchener, imperialist and soldier, who, on a special mission to Russia, drowned along with most of the crew of HMS *Hampshire* after it struck a mine. Local folk, who knew every inch of cliff and shore, hurried to give assistance to the few seamen who had managed to struggle ashore, but were prevented from doing so by the military. It was to be the old and obscene story of secrecy at any cost.

Earls Palace is an incongruous mass among a huddle of humble dwellings. A bastion of gun-loops, tall chimneys (seventeen, they reckon), fireplaces and flues, built by Robert Stewart, Earl of Orkney in the latter half of the sixteenth century. No ascetic, he, think I, as I wander through a desolation of roofless rooms, whose walls and ceilings glimmered once with fireflicker, wall hangings and decoratively painted panels of wood. A touchingly naive, though detailed seventeenth-century drawing of Earls Palace, held by the Scottish Record Office, shows landing stages for boats, peat stacks, herb and flower gardens, an archery area and bowling green.

A circular well in the centre of the courtyard inspires an apprehensive chorus of 'ooh's!' and 'ah's!' from a gabble of brightly-clad children.

Approximately four miles from the Palace, off the B9056, is a small firm with a deservedly spreading national reputation. I'm no real ale buff, but even my whisky-scoured palate can differentiate between the gaseous washing-up liquid we in Scotland know as beer, and the dark and malty brew at Orkney Brewers.

Civil engineer Roger White had had his fill of world travel when he chucked his job to set up business in a disused school in the parish of Sandwick. And no, he had never made beer in his life, before his three-week course in a Hampshire brewers, he told me, as I sampled a cool mid-morning draught of 100-shilling, Dark Island, in the equally cool, whitewashed interior of his tiny brewery.

'Good, eh!' he said, as my throat worked at the malty nectar. 'No chemicals or additives, there. Just hops from Worcestershire, malted barley from East Lothian and, as is the case also with Orkney's Highland Park whisky, excellent spring water ...' 'Plus a pinch or two of magic,' said I. He smiles coyly: 'There's that, too.'

I suspect success will force him to extend the business which he and his wife, Irene, and local lad, Alan Irvin, run so well. As

I write there are few, as yet, retail outlets outwith Orkney for his best-selling Raven Ale; famous not only for its flavour, but also for its distinctive raven logo on bottle and bar tap. I wish them luck.

I've heard tell there used to be as many Garsons in Orkney as there are coopats in a field o' coos. I'm proud of my surname. A third of the Garsons, I believe, live in the parish of Sandwick. From the old Norse *garor*: a wall or dyke that makes an enclosure, it is a common element in farm names long since shortened to *gar*, as in Brogar, Midgarth, etc. Old tunship (township) dykes were also known as garths; hence the common place-name Garson: *garos-endi*, dyke end.

An old friend insists that the film star, Greer Garson, is my late father's second cousin. The genealogical stew is further enriched by those film biographers who say her antecedents are Irish. Fact or myth? I don't know. But I'll boast of it at the drop of a bunnet. Well, I did, until I got speaking to a Sandwick woman one deserted winter's morning at the Bay of Skaill, who, deep into our bletherings, revealed that Greer Garson was second cousin to a member of *her* family. Confused — for I've never understood the complexities of lineage — I sprinkled my blessings on our day, and, filled with a sense of belonging, hummed an artless tune as I followed the shoreland path towards Skara Brae.

Skara Brae is the best known and best preserved subterranean Pictish village in Europe. Founded some five thousand years ago, the name, Skara Brae, or Skerrabrae, is derived from the sand dune which covered the site prior to 1850, when it was uncovered by a great storm. Perched as it is on the edge of the eroded shore, it would originally have been much further back from the sea. Evidence suggests that a freshwater loch may even have separated the site from the sandy shore.

The entire village is in a remarkably fine state of preservation, due to its protection from the elements by mounds of earth and domestic rubbish. It consists of six corbelled squarish stone huts or houses, linked by a confusion of covered subterranean passages. The contrast between those low passages and the lofty nine-feet high interiors of the living quarters catches the visitor unawares, and is reminiscent of the stooped, then fully-stretched structure of Maeshowe, and other similar burial cairns.

The housing units, though smoke-filled and uncomfortable by our interior-sprung standards, must have been very cosy, hung, as they would have been, with animal skins and furs, the floors and beds strewn with heather. It is the domestic furniture however, which fascinates the first-time visitor: the stone slab dressers built against the walls, the slab-sided beds, drains and lavatories, the hearth with stone kerbs in the centre of the floor, and the watertight stone boxes set into the floor for the storage of live shellfish.

That they were a close-knit, even comfortably off community of farmers, fishers, toolmakers and potters, seems more than likely.

An average of 47,000 tourists a year descend on Skara Brae, the custodian told me, squaring his shoulders, as the first of the days bright straggle wound along the bay's edge.

It's like an adventure playground here, at the height of the season. I've even caught folk stealing stones from the walls, to take home as souvenirs. Then there are those who think they should be allowed in for free, because they happen to be a friend of so-an-so. There are good people, too, mind you. People who care and are really interested in what I have to say. The rest never fail to surprise me.

The village of Dounby straddles the boundaries of three parishes, some five miles inland from Bay of Skaill. It is the hub of this rich farming area. And the host of August's West Mainland cattle show. A restored example of a water mill, once common to Orkney, can be seen at Click Mill, just south of Dounby.

The parish of Stenness is particularly dear to me. Layered with evocations of times past. A time of which the Orcadian writer and poet, Edwin Muir, in *An Autobiography* writes:

The farmers did not know ambition and the petty torments of ambition; they did not realize what competition was, though they lived at the end of Queen Victoria's reign; they helped one another with their work when help was required, following the old usage; they had a culture made up of legend, folk song, and the poetry and prose of the Bible; they had customs which sanctioned their instinctive feelings for the earth; their life was an order, and a good order.

It was around the tail-end of such a culture that I met Davo. The world was dipping its toe into the tides of war. Davo Craigie, crofter, lived with his wife Annabella and grandson John, in an exposed cottage on the shore of Stenness, between the Bay of Ireland and Clestrain Sound. The cramped stone-flagged living room-cum-kitchen, was furnished with five hard chairs and a scrubbed deal table. A butter churn sulked in a dark corner. Against the reek-stained wall, a dresser: a shrine to Christmasses past emblazoned with biscuit tin icons of kittens and puppies and paunchy pipe majors, skirling fit to burst. Peats cut from April's fudgy moorlands smouldered at the heart of the black-leaded cooking range, above which, hung smoked shanks of pig.

He was a short and wiry, walrus moustached and perma-nently bunneted seventy-year old ex merchant seaman, who laughed a lot. A weaver of endless yarns, and a perceptive though gentle critic of the follies and fashions of city folks Soothaboots.

I have vivid memories of him scything in the low field, against a noonday shimmer of sea and sky, as I negotiated my bike down the track leading to his scatter of dykes and steadings. We'd shake hands, calm the collie and walk towards the croft. Annabella chattered nervously. John swayed from foot-to-foot, assessing me all the while beneath his lowered bunnet peak.

After I'd had my fill of strong tea, cheese and bannocks, I'd steer him round, laddie-like, towards the fishing. For no matter how many peats he may have cut, or how difficult his rain-flattened crops had been to scythe that day, Davo, provided the sea was good, invariably took me on the water of an evening, for a bit fun with the cuithes (two or three-year-old coal-fish). The rod for this type of sea fishing is no more than a long bamboo cane, known as a *wand* (pronounced *waand*). A few feet of line interspersed with hooks bound with tufts of seagull or duck feathers attached to a heavy gut cast, is lashed to the tip, and trailed from the stern of a rowing boat. It's as simple as that.

The pre-fishing rituals were unbearably unhurried. The best wand was selected from a stinking tangle behind the lobby door, dull lures replaced by fresh, white ones, and splits lashed with twine, whilst Annabella — ever caring — rummaged and raked along a line of working coats and jackets, '... for it can be gey caald on the sea, boy.'

Afloat now, he'd lay a thin plank of wood across the gunwale, tell me to sit on it facing the stern, put the wand in my hand and pull away from the shallows, towards an otherworld, where ribbons of black and crimson seaweed hung motionless in the slack tide.

A shimmer of sand eels darted beneath the keel, seaweeds began to sway, crabs scuttled, limpets gripped, lobsters flexed gunmetal claws, and I'd be on to cuithes! Throwing themselves at the hooks, two and three at a time. Soon, dozens, flashing silver, clattering open-gobbed at Davo's feet. My heart thumping, scrawny arms aching.

It would stop as suddenly as it had started, my line trailing slackly astern. 'There'll be no more fish this night,' he'd say, pulling strongly for the shore. A chill breeze roughening the seas calm.

After beaching the dinghy, then threading my slippery harvest with coarse twine, I'd carry them with pride into the warm room. Annabella, selecting eight of the best, split them, raked out the pink innards with her thumb, and fried them for supper. The remainder would be gutted then strung along the outside wall to dry in the wind and sun, until they snapped between the fingers. After which they were stored. Soaked in warm water, then boiled and eaten with potatoes, they made a good and nutritious winter's meal.

I recall, too, a shared harvest dinner at their home, where, along with two boiled hens, the potatoes were timmed from the pot onto the centre of the wooden table. Neither fork nor spoon was used as hosts and neighbours selected, peeled and dipped the floury jacket potatoes in a bowl of melted butter, and stripped portions of bird from the steaming mound.

I think of them, constantly.

The tiny round church just off the A964 in the parish of Orphir, overlooking Scapa Flow, is probably the oldest surviving ecclesiastical ruin in Orkney. Only the half-barrel ceiling of the apse with traces of the original plaster, and a fragment of the unique circular nave remain. Its location next to the excavated walls of Earl Hakon's Hall (he who was responsible for the slaying of Magnus) make it a site of great historical importance.

Built in the first half of the twelfth century and dedicated to St Nicholas, its circular plan was inspired by the Church of the Holy Sepulchre in Jerusalem, during the time of the Crusades. The tragedy is that, this simple masterpiece was partly demolished in 1757, and its masonry recycled to build a new parish church next to it, which, in its turn, was demolished completely.

Active limbs could do worse than climb Ward Hill of Orphir; wee brother to Ward Hill of Hoy across the water, which is near double the height at 1,565 feet, and steeper by far. Ward is a common name reserved for the highest hills in Orkney, most of which were used as lookout and beacon points throughout Orkney's dishevelled history.

The summit of Wideford Hill to the east, is another top worth the puff. I don't normally rave about scenic *views* as such, and won't, but the ones from this wind-cuffed mound are truly something to rave about.

On the downhill daudle I make tracks for Wideford Hill Cairn: a tiny though beautifully constructed rectangular burial chamber, where it's down the hatch, literally.

31

CHAPTER THREE
East Mainland

There are three parishes on East Mainland: Holm (pronounced Ham), St Andrews, and Deerness east of the narrow peninsular. There are few dramatic vistas, though sophisticated eyes will draw pleasure from the heather and farm-strewn horizons. And city drivers, weaned on curses, will enjoy the straight and smoothly tarred A960.

Approximately four miles out of Kirkwall, take the left-hander past Kirkwall airport, and follow the road skirting the peninsula between Inganess Bay and Deer Sound. The area surrounding Hall of Tankerness, country seat of the Baikies, and one of Orkney's richest seventeenth century families, is worth exploring. As is the shoreline east of Loch of Tankerness. There's splendid rock and cave scenery along the east coast, with names to match: Hangie Bay, Gumpick, Hole of Roe, Taing of Beeman.

Readers of the Norse Sagas will be familiar with the word, *thing* (local public assemblies for law and legislation, in short, parliaments) from which are derived the words *ting*, as in Tingwall in Rendall, and *ding*, as in Dingwall, on the Cromarty Firth. Tynwald in the Isle of Man is another. One such parliament or *thing* assembled, it is thought, at the huge mound of Dingieshowe (the *thing* mound), which can be seen to the right, as you enter the narrow isthmus between Dingyshowe Bay and Sandi Sound. It is no surprise that, given the strategic nature of the land, the broch builders placed a fort on the lip of the shore.

Nearby Newark Bay is white of sand, turquoise of sea and is typical of Orkney's many beaches. One local told me that, if Orkney was several hundred miles south of the Pentland Firth, and subsequently warmer, it would be another Blackpool. My skin crept at the thought.

A reliable source claims to have seen a fair quantity of

old human bones embedded in the eroded banks above the shoreline of this bay, but I never found them.

The Skaill road in the parish of Deerness, ends at the car park, a short step from one of the most awesome of geological phenomena this side of Gustave Dorés illustrations to Dante's vision of Hell and Purgatory.

J. Gunn, author of *Orkney the Magnetic North*, says it all: 'A cave where there is an upward slope in the rock strata, may rise gradually some distance above the level of its entrance. Sometimes the roof of the inner part of the cave then collapses, leaving a great open pit above the inner end of the tunnel. Such a pit is known as a *gloup* (pronounced gloop). The length of the tunnel may be fifty yards or more, and the diameter of the gloup as much, while the depth may be eight or a hundred feet, according to the height of the cliff: a gloup has a weird, uncanny air. The surface of the ground gives no warning of its presence. Suddenly the visitor finds himself on the brink of a vast pit with perpendicular walls of rock, and with the sea foam, it may be, crawling about in its gloomy depth. It might well suggest connection with the underworld rather than with the sunny sparkling sea so close to hand.'

The Gloup of Deerness is one such abyss: 60 to 70 feet deep, some 150 yards in length, and, for me, doubly menacing on days of quiet calm when the amplified sighs and sniggerings of an idle sea drift upwards from the great soundbox. There's a perfectly safe and robust visitors viewing platform. So, if Icarus like, you fall into the frothy cauldron, you've only yourself to blame. Take heed of Orkney Island Council's warning notice at the car park!

The small and uninhabited island of Copinsay to the south east, is a bird reserve in memory of the anthropologist, James Fisher, and is one of the most important sea bird sites in Orkney. Largely undisturbed by humans, the high cliffs were harvested in the not so distant past, for sea birds and eggs. The climbers being lowered by horse-hair ropes handled by their mates on the crag's rim.

Copinsay is also the home of trolls, or trows, those super-natural creatures of Scandinavian folklore. Stories of which,

Ernest W. Marwick tells with chilling conviction in his fascinating *The Folklore of Orkney and Shetland*.

When the mood takes me, I like to top the day with a bracing coastal tramp to the Brough of Deerness, and its barely discernible twelfth century chapel ruin which, some say, can be reached by a narrow, almost inaccessible and extremely dangerous path. Wise travellers never get that near the peninsular's edge to find out.

Keen walkers will enjoy the bold and craggy Mull Head to the north, before making tracks across rough grassland towards Scarva Taing and the memorial erected in 1888 to the memory of some 250 Scottish Covenanters who, bound for transportation as slaves to the American colonies, were shipwrecked on the Scarva Taing rocks.

After the aborted rising by the Covenanters at Bothwell Bridge in 1679, over one thousand men were imprisoned for months in the grounds of Greyfriars Churchyard, Edinburgh. Many died by starvation, exposure and the rope. Some submitted to episcopacy and the English Book of Common Prayer and were freed. The remaining two hundred and fifty prisoners were shipped from the port of Leith onboard the barque, *Crown*, and battened down in the tiny, black hold.

It is thought that Patterson, the captain, intended to make Mull Head his first landfall, when a storm forced him to anchor off Scirva Taing, not far from the safer anchorage of Deer Sound. The storm rose, driving the *Crown* on to the Scirva Taing rocks. The captain and crew made it to dry land, but most of the prisoners were left to drown at the captain's command, 'Batten down the hatches and let the dogs die.'

Examples of burnt mounds can be seen nearby, and are clearly indicated on the Ordnance Survey map of the area. A common phenomenan in the Northern Isles, Wales and Southern Ireland, but rare in Scotland, they are literally mounds, mostly grassed over, of burnt and split stones, and are always located at a nearby source of fresh water.

They were in fact prehistoric kitchens, some no doubt communal. A pit lined with stone slabs, was filled with water, brought to the boil, and kept at boiling point by the continuous immersion of red-hot stones. This way, slabs of meat, often on the hide, were boiled. After which, the stones were discarded round the cooking area — hence burnt mounds. Although the roasting of meat was a common practice, a great deal of nutritious fat would be lost in the process. Boiling not only retained most of the fat, but also made for a more succulent meal.

CHAPTER FOUR

Kirkwall

Five roads converge on Kirkwall, all of which, common to most cathedral towns, thrill with tantalizing glimpses of tower and steeple.

It is not known who first settled in this naturally bielded haven ... Picts, probably. The present town layout masks the original medieval village which lay on the edge of the Peerie (small) Sea, which was much larger than today's road-girt pond to the west. Excavations have shown that the sea was within yards of the cathedral in the twelfth century, prior to the reclaiming of the land with rubble, earth and shingle, in the thirteenth century.

That the place is well sheltered from March winds is obvious, when viewed from the brink of any one of the approach roads. Here then, was a safe (well, safe-ish) place for early settlers to fish from frail coracles, fatten herds, hunt, break land with mattock and plough.

It was here, too, that the Christian missionaries came in the fourth century, fired by the zeal and inspiration of Ninian, who built at Whithorn in Wigtownshire, a stone church known as *Ad Candidam Casam*: 'At the White House'. References in Orkneyinga Saga show also that there were Viking Age settlements in Kirkwall before and during the tenth century.

The church which preceded St Magnus Cathedral, and which gave Kirkwall (Kirkjuvagr: church bay) its name, was St Olafs Church built by Earl Rognvald Brusison, in honour of his foster father, King Olaf Haraldsson — St Olaf. All that remains of this early Latin and Catholic church, is a weathered doorway with traces of nailhead decoration, in St Olaf's Wynd — formerly Poorhouse Close — off Bridge Street. And a hogback tombstone in Tankerness House Museum.

St Magnus Cathedral was built by Earl Rognvald Kolsson a century after the building of St Olaf's Church, and was dedicated

to his martyred uncle, Magnus, who was treacherously mur-
dered in Easter Week, 1115, on the island of Egilsay. He was
canonised twenty years later. After which, his remains were
transferred, some sources say, to the tiny Christ Church on the
Brough of Birsay, before their interment in the large rectangular
pier of the south arcade of the choir of St Magnus Cathedral,
where they remain to this day.

Due no doubt to the prestigious nature of the cathedral,
which was under way from 1137, other settlements spawned
along the shore southwards of the Peerie Sea. A bishop and
an earl's palace were erected and Kirkwall became two towns
— the earls and the bishop's — the natives of which didn't
always live in harmony one with the other. Their boundaries
are marked by what is now Post Office Lane.

It is tempting to think that the old town division continues
to this day in the form of the Ba' Game (ball game), which
takes place on Christmas day and New Year's day. Those who
come from the north part of the town are called Doonies; those
from the south, Uppies. Two games are played by boys in the
morning, and men in the afternoon. There are no rules, teams
as such, or referees. Each side can have as many players (a
misnomer for barbarians) as it wants. The aim: to boot, blooter
and hurl the leather ball into the Down-the Gate's harbour, or
Up-the Gate's goal at Mackinson's Corner. Imagine a rugby
scrum of some 150 men, sans rulebook and ref, locked head
to shoulder, hair matted and steaming, none of them prepared
to yield an inch, surging through the narrow-gutted window
barricaded streets.

That the Ba' Game has its origins in Norse times is probable,
as a similar game, *Knattleikr*, is described in the Saga of Gisli.

The town was occupied by Cromwell's troops during the civil
war. The cathedral was used as horse stables, with little damage
to its fabric; and a fort was erected on the shoreline. It was a
relatively benign occupation by all accounts. An apocryphal
hand-me-down claims that his — Cromwell's — troopers,
even went as far as dispensing gardening tips to the natives.
Hmm . . .

In the eighteenth century, trade with foreign parts burgeoned, mainly from potash made from burned kelp: a large brown seaweed used in the manufacture of glass and iodine. Farming methods improved, and Kirkwall's status as a port of exportation of farm produce was known throughout Britain.

Kirkwall today, unlike its more linear neighbour, Stromness, is a straggle of walled lanes and back streets, scattered like shattered spokes around the hub of the cathedral. Approximately one third of Orkney's population live here, the number of which has almost trebled since 1821, when the total was 2,600.

That the place is Orkney's capital, is obvious. There's Woolworths, candy-pink with goodies. Shoe shops, banks, estate agents, hotels, and people-bright harbour bars thrumming with boasts and banter and tales of times that never were. And a chippy in Bridge Street with chips like wot they used to be: hot, hand cut and multi-formed on a foundation of crispy bits, topped by a stiff dollop of tomato sauce (I abhor those cloned and computerised cones of pallid French fries). The County Library at the head of Laing Street, founded in 1683, is the oldest public library in Scotland, and a splendid haven, that not only caters for the general reader, but also houses a collection of old books, maps and photographs of old Orkney, in the appropriately named Orkney Room. Explore, too, the harbour area: haven for yachts, small craft, liberty boat landing stage for well upholstered liner passengers, and berth of the excellent Orkney Islands Shipping Companie's ferries which serve the North Isles.

Victoria Street, south of the cathedral, unlike the more business like ambience of Broad Street and Albert Street to the north, like Stromness, has a Scandinavian feel to it, but lacks that town's unheralded arrowslit seaviews. It begins at Victoria Hall, where THE WORD OF THE LORD ENDURETH FOR EVER, and ends at the symmetrical façade of Kirkwall Baptist Church: GLORY TO GOD IN THE HIGHEST. Between those trumpeted homilies, time-warped shops go about their daily business. Reassuring places staffed by bright and kindly assistants, well-versed in the quality and purpose of their wares: thermal drawers and Wolsey jerseys, socks, gloves, mittens and

Tootal ties. In the window, a luggy cap with a wind-cheater lining, stout boots, donkey jackets, boiler suits and dungarees on rigor-mortis dummies. A tiny shoe shop, its door ajar, emits smells of leather spiced with beeswax. And the baker's window is dressed overall with a temptation of bannocks, pies, cakes and varnished buns.

Though blackened and stunted now, it's good to see that The Big Tree in Albert Street has been — by popular and vehement public demand — granted stay of execution by the powers that be, and that sparse though defiant twigs sprout still. For this is no ordinary tree, but a national totem in a land largely devoid of trees — except for that bizarre and scrawny wood in Finstown. 'This is the *only* tree in the *whole* of Orkney,' my father would say, as I gawped with childish wonder at its dark green and luxuriant crown.

To find a twelfth-century cathedral of such splendour, among a scattered fistful of islands is wonder indeed. Although it should be remembered that Kirkwall, at that time, was at the centre of the north European trade routes. That it exists this far north of Durham's Transitional masterpiece, is as good a reason as any for visiting Orkney. For this is no dour, begrimed kirk, the likes of which squat grudgingly at the heart of some Scottish towns and cities.

I'm what the late Alec Clifton-Taylor calls an 'amateur of churches'. In southern parts, especially, I've only to catch a glimpse of some Norman parish church tower, and I hurry to it like a pubescent lover. Harold Nicolson puts it better:

> Even if Hell exists (which I doubt), and even if Heaven is a reality (which I sincerely hope is not true), ... I believe that the gift I most appreciate is the gift of seeing beauty. Why should I experience such a spurt of pleasure at seeing the tower of Staplehurst Church catch the sun through fog?

Orkney was under Norse rule throughout the building of St Magnus Cathedral. Though founded in 1137, and in all probability designed and built by experienced English and Scottish craftsmen, the people of Orkney waited long for its completion: hence the mixture of architectural styles from

Romanesque (rounded and chunky), to Transitional (pointy and Gothic).

The Orkneyinga Saga relates that the momentum to build the new church came, not from the body of the church, but from Kol Kalason; Norwegian chieftain and comrade of Earl Rognvald, thus:

> We've heard reports from Orkney that everyone there wants to stand up against you and defend the realm beside Earl Paul. They'll be slow to abandon the hatred fostered against you, kinsman. Now here's my advice: look for support where men will say the true owner of the realm granted it to you, and that's the holy Earl Magnus, your uncle. I want you to make a vow to him, that should he grant you your family inheritance and his own legacy, and should you come to power, then you'll build a stone minster at Kirkwall more magnificent than any in Orkney, that you'll have it dedicated to your uncle the holy Earl Magnus and provide it with all the funds it will need to flourish. In addition, his holy relics and the episcopal seat must be moved there.

He succeeded, of course; took over the earldom and set about building his great church.

Before entering the interior, I take time to explore the west front and graveyard setting beyond Kirk Green, formerly the town's market place, for there are architectural riches and sculptured details in abundance ... binoculars come in handy here. Particularly fine are the three thirteenth-century west front doorways with their polychrome, almost Moorish use of alternate red and white stone. The red, of which, was quarried — dare I say it? — a stone's throw from Kirkwall, at Carness. The whitish yellow, from the island of Eday. Good examples of the stone carver's art can be seen also on the delicately ornate heads of the capitals of the shafted jambs on one of the lesser doorways. An example, perhaps, of the use of the mason's chisel which superseded the old stonecarving axe? Search, too, for the gey worse for wear but delightful twinned mermaids.

A wealth of quirky detail can be found elsewhere: the rows of malevolent and misbegotten carved heads, plus interesting wee north and south doors. The original spire, destroyed by fire in 1671, was replaced by a squat pyramidal one, which was subsequently replaced shortly before the First World War by the mock Gothic copper thrust we see today. I'm not alone in thinking it a pretentious substitute for its dumpy predecessor which, according to contemporary prints and photographs, was in keeping with the overall style.

Fewer things give me a buzz of expectancy more than pushing open a cathedral door. I hold my breath, step into the initial gloom, sniff candle wax, crysanthemums, and a hint of damp, and hunch in awe as I adjust to the divine theatricality of stone and glass. I have my favourites, of course; those which yield endless riches of mass and detail and ever-shifting moods of light. I think of the overwhelming transept of Ely; the Norman nave and fifteenth-century vault of Norwich; the leaded glass of Chartres, York and Canterbury, and the chevroned voussoirs of St Cuthbert's, that tiny Norman masterpiece at Dalmeny, near South Queensferry. But it is the unexpected scale and muscular grandeur of St Magnus Cathedral which grips the imagination.

Like the cathedrals of Norwich and Durham, it is a happy amalgam of the outgoing, fortified Romanesque style, and that of the incoming, more rarified Gothic style, unspoiled (well, almost unspoiled) by modifications and enlargements according to the fashion of the age.

First impressions are, that this is a large and lofty interior space. The overall length, however (I'm too old to learn new tricks, so I'll give it to you in feet and inches), is a mere 217 feet 10 inches; width of choir and aisles at east end, 47 feet 5½ inches; width of choir and nave between pillars, 16 feet 9 inches; width across transept, 89 feet 6 inches; height to the vaulting, 71 feet; height of tower and spire, 150 feet. In short, a perfect balance between length, breadth and height.

That the red and white sandstone lend character and drama to the overall effect is obvious. But — and no one drools more over weel biggit [well built] stonework than I — I can't help but doubt the 'improving' urges which drove our Victorian and post-Victorian forebears to strip Britain's ancient churches of their plaster rendering; some of which retained their original decorations, abstract and figurative, beneath the smoorings of limewash: '... skinning a church alive', as William Morris so aptly put it. For up to the Victorian period rubblestone walls, and dressed ashlar even, were rendered or limewashed, and never meant to be seen. And St Magnus Cathedral, in my view, suffers in part from the same spotty-dotty, busy surfaces common to a great many of our ecclesiastical houses.

Despite that, St Magnus is the only cathedral I can most readily envisage in its original state: the walls lined out with painted imitation jointing, cinquefoils, stars, martyrs and saints, picked out in ochre, red, lime white, lamp and charcoal black. Down the nave, a fanfare of banners. And windows of stained and leaded glass. The apse, lambent with embroidered silks, precious metals and stones. The reek of incense, fish oil and tallow candle permeating plaster, timber and penitential stone-flagged floor.

Thankfully, common sense and multifarious cultural events such as the annual St Magnus Festival prevent the likelihood of ruining the nave with the drear and dreaded fixed kirk pew. For there's nowt like it to deaden the proportions of a fine cathedral — unless it's the equally dreaded Victorian pipe organ.

It grieves me though, that this nobly austere church harbours a plethora of far from noble Victorian and post Victorian features. I think here of the inappropriate stained glass windows with their overworked and inert symbols of religiosity; the fussy alter floor; the banal St Rognvald's Chapel; the ectoplasmic white marble memorial at the choir aisle. Yes, it's a problem, I know, but imaginatively sympathetic and gutsy early and late twentieth-century church art does exist: see Durham Cathedral's Galilee Chapel; Fernand Leger's *dalle-de-verre* windows at Audincourt; the leaded glass of Evie Hone in Farm Street Church, London.

My plus points go to an invigorating, head-on seventeenth-century celebration of death and resurrection in the form of the Mort Brod — a wooden memorial which hangs in the nave; the tombstones of the same period, the fiercely moustached carved heads in choir and aisle, the fist-sized stone carving of the Green Man (that beneficient spirit of vegetation), the blind arcading, the rigid, axe and orb-bearing polychromed St Olaf, and other things brave, in this boldly faceted garnet in Orkney's crown.

Little remains of the twelfth-century palace, built, it is thought, by William the Old; bishop and Viking longboat captain ... now, there's *real* versatility for you. Traces of the original building can be seen in the stonework in the lower part of the building. It was on this site that King Hakon Hakonsson, a guest of the bishop, died in the autumn of 1263 after his calamitious skirmish with the Scots at the battle of Largs. Most of the ruin you see today dates from Bishop Reid's reconstruction of 1541–8; the distinctive part of which is the fortified round tower, for these were hostile times. Reid, however, was a most competent and respected Scottish statesman, founder of the University of Edinburgh, financier and scholar. He was also one of four commissioners who attended the wedding of Mary Queen of Scots to the Dauphin. Homeward bound, all four took ill and died at Dieppe of poison. Though whether from dodgy continental shellfish or an assassin's hand, no one knows.

Legend has it that it was here, in the Bishop's Palace, that King Robert the Bruce was sheltered after his defeat by the Earl of Pembroke at the battle of Methven Park, near Perth, in 1306. After overwintering there, and when spring came, he made his way down the Western Isles assisted by his Norse friends and comrades-in-arms.

The bloody era of the old Norse earls was as nothing, compared to the long humiliating years of Scottish domination. Orkney hoatched with peripatetic chancers, wide-boy specu- lators and assorted miscreants fleeing from the short arm of the law. The rights of the people were not only abused by the powers that were, but eventually abolished.

In 1565, Robert Stewart, an illegitimate son of James the Fifth and half brother of the ubiquitous Mary Queen of Scots, was rewarded with the earldom, of which, his son, Earl Patrick Stewart inherited during his father's lifetime. J. Gunn, in his excellent *Orkney the Magnetic North*, describes their characters thus:

> ... the rapacity and oppression and sheer illegalities practised by these two, father and son, were such that their names have lived on in the

tradition as those of evil spirits incarnate. Lands were confiscated, fines were unjustly extorted, compulsory services exacted, and no form of oppression was omitted which might gratify their shameless cupidity.

The ruin of Earl Patrick's Palace squats on barbered lawns. Blackbirds dib and dab. A determination of gnarled trees enliven the bland aspect common to most tourist attractions. Built by slave labour around 1600, the palace is an imposing — experts say the finest — example of Scottish Renaissance secular architecture extant. And, ruin though it is, one can imagine the indulgent lifestyle of its incumbent: the feasts in the great hall, the sycophants at the top table, the thin strains of virginal and viol, the sudden drink-taken brawl.

His come-uppance at the hands of the Church, in the form of new man, Bishop James Law, must have heartened the severely oppressed people of Orkney. Brought to trial for his wrongdoings, Earl Patrick, or *Black Pate* as he was aptly dubbed, was jailed, convicted and beheaded at the Market Cross in Edinburgh in February 1615.

Nearby Tankerness House in Broad Street — originally the subchantry and archdeanery for the cathedral — was the winter house of the Baikie's; merchant lairds and one of Orkneys oldest families, the last of whom sold up and emigrated at the end of World War Two.

Now a museum, this fine sixteenth-century town house is well worth visiting, both for is architectural charm and its contents. Though for me, who prefers our museums to be higgledy-piggledy, laconically informative, and romantically fousty, the displays seem slightly self-conscious and clinical.

There are good things to mull over in the courtyard mill and quern stones, sculptured bits-and-bobs, plus a fragment of hogback coffin. Inside there's a good introductory set piece: 'The First Settlers'. A convincing reconstruction of a section of Skara Brae; the stone dresser filled with imitation meat and fish and a gathering of driftwood. And a dramatically lit arrangement of skulls from the Tomb of the Eagles, Isbister.

Upstairs in an enchantment of creaky-floored and lop-sided rooms, can be seen the coffin-cum-kist which housed the remains of St Magnus prior to his interment in the large rectangular pier of the south arcade of the cathedral choir. An accompanying black and white photograph of his axe-split skull adds credence to the drama. There's a crisply incised Pictish symbol stone for good measure. And a covetous medieval stone carving of Magnus, the saint, weather-buffed and incongruous in the small centrally heated room.

Ola Gorrie, jeweller, is an affable woman who smiles readily, wears good, though far from ostentatious clothes, and carries her international success with the kind of ease that invariably masks years of struggle.

After studying at Gray's School of Art, Aberdeen, in the fifties, she began work in a shed at the back of her parent's home in 1960, and, she told me, has been 'adding to that ever since'.

It was to be a long haul from that to her present, newly extended and sophisticated Broad Street manufacturing premises: the outcome of a fairly recent £450,000 expansion programme (part financed by Highlands and Islands Enterprise), which will bring the workforce up to 39 full- and part-time staff.

It is a professionally and happily run ship, steered by her managing director husband, Arnold, and their sons, Neil and Shawn, who manage the shop and the practicalities of the workshop, respectively. A daughter, Ingrid, runs her own business as a designer of scarves and shawls.

And if all that sounds a mite too smart to those precious, one-off fashioners of things crafty, they couldn't be more wrong. For folks, after all, have been producing multiples of flawless beauty from moulds, ever since man discovered how to smelt metals.

'The quality of my mother's designs starts here,' said Shawn, introducing me to Colin Watson who makes the master patterns. 'Great care and time is taken at this stage to ensure that Colin's interpretation of the original sketch design is just so, before it goes through the moulding, casting and finishing processes.'

And again, if that has a clinical ring to it, it couldn't be further from the truth. For multiples though they are, Gorrie's translations in gold and silver, of bird, beast, plant form and ancient stone carving are as fresh and as lively as you'll find, wherever there are artists who care about their works. It's called class.

I have an aversion to guided tours in general, but enjoyed the one at Highland Park Distillers, Holm Road. Not only because I'm a fair imbiber of the amber potion — Highland Park 12-year-old in particular — but also because of the witty and light delivery of American-born guide, Day Wishart, who shepherded her charges through a wonderland of burnished copper stills, mashvats, hogsheads and butts. The malty aromas of barley mash curling round my heart. Taste buds alert with expectation.

Visitors are treated to a wee snifter of the nectar at the end of the tour. I sloped off for a large one, with a Murphy's chaser at my favourite, smoke-fugged harbour bar. Cheers!

CHAPTER FIVE

Across the Churchill Barriers

One autumn morning in 1918, the scrag end of the German High Sea Fleet, stripped of guns, pennants and similarly obvious signs of power, and manned by skeleton crews, steamed slowly into Scapa Flow under an escort of the British Grand Fleet. It was to be the last anchorage of thirteen battleships, five battle cruisers and fifty destroyers, and the stage set for the ignominious end to the proudest and second largest naval fleet in the world.

At 9.a.m. on Saturday 21 June 1919, the Battle Squadron of the British Grand Fleet left Scapa Flow with attendant destroyers for North Sea manoeuvres ... the cat was away! Then, at 10.30.a.m. precisely, Admiral Von Reuter signalled to put into immediate operation his pre-arranged plan to scuttle the German fleet.

It was at that precise hour that a party of Stromness Secondary School pupils on a tour of the German fleet on board the fleet water-boat *Flying Kestrel*, witnessed something they would never forget, as the German ships suddenly and slowly sank, or turned turtle in up to twenty-five fathoms of water. Some bairns, I gather, thought that this show to end all shows was put on specifically for their entertainment.

Naval salvage teams refloated those ships which were beached or had sunk in shallow water. Partly submerged wrecks were stripped by local squads for the value of scrap metal and souvenirs; some of which were shipped from Orkney in herring barrels to lucrative southern markets.

Later salvage operations by various salvage syndicates were many and varied in sophistication. Notable was the firm of Cox and Danks, who raised twenty-five destroyers by a unique system of powerful winches and pulleys, allied to a huge floating dock. After which, dock and destroyer were towed into shallow water, beached, then winched inland. Others were raised by compressed air and air balloons. The risks to diver and salvage crews beggar description.

A *Daily Mail* correspondent of 14 August 1926, on board the raised hulk of the battlecruiser *Hindenburg*, wrote:

> Skeletons of easy chairs float in the barber's shop and a big mirror gave me a somewhat dull reflection ... heavy cups hang in orderly rows from the ceiling of the officers' serving room. Everything of metal, wood or porcelain is still unbroken and usable despite seven year's submersion.

A precisely crafted silver sugar bowl stamped ART. KRUPP. BERNDORF., salvaged from *Hindenburg's* officer's saloon by a friend of my father, sits on my desk, stuffed with staples, pens, an eraser and other odds-and-ends of my questionable trade.

An excellent wee booklet, *The Salving of the German Fleet*, by J. Pottinger, published by Stromness Museum, describes fully this triumph of engineering skills and human perseverance.

There are few who haven't heard of Scapa Flow; Orkney's great, roughly diamond-shaped sea heaven. Age-old anchorage for Viking longship, barque and brigantine, and the furtive grey ships of two world wars. It was here, too, in a landlocked finger of sea beyond the coast of Gaitnip, that one of the most tragic, though most daring of wartime naval episodes took place at the outset of World War Two.

It seemed extremely unlikely to the powers that were that German vessels of any description could penetrate any one of the narrow channels leading into the Flow. Deliberately blocked as they were during the First World War by wrecked ships — *block ships* — which, in turn, had the effect of increasing the power and danger of the already fearsome tide rips. It was unlikely therefore, and near as dammit impossible that German submarines would slither into Scap Flow from that end.

They hadn't, however, reckoned for the daring and near visionary seamanship of one, Kapitänleutnant Günther Prien of U-47 who, on the night of the 13 October 1939, managed to penetrate a gap between the block ships and net booms in the narrows of Holm Sound, torpedoed the battleship *Royal*

Oak at anchor in the Flow, then turned tail back the way he had come.

She sank rapidly, with the loss of 833 men. There were no civilian witnesses.

The wreck of the *Royal Oak* lies below the cliffs of Gaitnip in ninety-eight feet of water, and is an official war grave marked by a large green buoy. It is prohibited to skin divers.

It was Winston Churchill whose idea it was to close completely those vulnerable gaps once and for all. Early experiments failed, as loads of stone and rubble were washed away by strong tides. He, Churchill, then came up with the idea of using large concrete blocks, each weighing anything from five to ten tons apiece, seventy thousand in all laid with great care and precision on a foundation of boulders. It was to be a difficult undertaking, with fierce tides and water up to ten fathoms deep to contend with. But with the combined skills of Italian prisoners of war and Orcadian and Scottish civilians under contract, a road was finally laid over. They called it *The Churchill Barriers*. It had taken four years to complete, at a total cost of two million pounds — and the lives of ten men.

What was formerly a hazardous pre-war boat trip for south islanders is now a delightful (though dodgy in strong winds) and hassle-free car run through a graduated necklace of islands: Lamb Holm, Glimps Holm, Burray and South Ronaldsay — the larger of the four.

The barriers begin at St Mary's in the Mainland parish of Holm. Formerly a fishing port, it is now a pleasant though undistinguished straggle of old indigenous and modern so-so.

Lamb Holm, the first gem in the string, is a small almond-shaped island, made famous by the tiny church known as the Italian Chapel, and is all that remains of Camp 60 which housed over five hundred Italian prisoners of war captured in the Western Desert during the North African Campaign. The camp consisted of some fifteen or so corrugated iron Nissen huts (named after Lt.Col. Peter Nissen, British mining engineer). Through time, flower beds, paths, a theatre, a recreation hut with a concrete billiard table and other humanizing influences appeared. The chapel — a born-again Nissen hut dedicated to

Regina Pacis, the Queen of Peace — was largely the brainchild of prisoner of war, Domenico Chiocchetti, bolstered by the goodwill of camp commandant, Major T.P. Buckland, and army padre, Fr. P. Gioachino Giacobazzi.

Though of no outstanding artistic merit, the chapel is nevertheless a work of considerable ingenuity, born from spiritual need, racial memory, and a transformation of scrap metal, plaster board, barbed wire, cement and sea-salvaged timber.

After the war its condition gradually deteriorated, and committees were formed to initiate minor repairs. In March 1960, however, Chiocetti, his travelling expenses met by the BBC, returned to his creation, and with the assistance of Kirkwall man, Stanley Hall, carried out general repairs, and restored much of the decorative paintwork. On the last Sunday of his visit, 10 April 1960, a service of re-dedication in the chapel was attended by two hundred Orcadians.

It is a most popular tourist attraction. Orkney Islands Council, sources tell me, are looking into the possibility of taking over the responsibility for its preservation and maintenance. I hope so.

From here on, it's a short and straight coastal run through Glimps Holm — small, pear-shaped and fertile — towards Barrier No. Three and the dog-leg roads of Burray, second largest island in the group of four.

I like Burray. The sweetly-curved and unexpected white sandy bay of South Links, between Black Rock and Kirk Taing. The village, pier, inn and boatyard stitched to the hem of Water Sound. And Hunda, attached umbilically by the roughly-cobbled sheep and pedestrian only concrete causeway of Hunda Reef.

The name Burray originates from the site of two Brochs — *borgarey* — and was known as Brochs Island, which was later abbreviated to Burray. It measures approximately four miles from east to west, and two miles from north to south, and was formerly the property of the Stewart family, who lived at the house known as the Bu of Burray. A contumelious and loutish lot, by all accounts, Sir James, it is said, was the only man out of Orkney to join Charles Edward Stuarts Jacobite Rebellion of

1745. After which, he managed to dodge the punitive intentions of the English, after the Battle of Culloden, then high-tailed it back to Burray, where he was eventually captured and shunted south to die in an English prison.

The name, Duncan, is synonymous in Burray parts with quality boat building, boat repairs and boat hiring. Although brothers Robin and Anthony Duncan have, on their own admission, known busier and better times, the yard ticks over on 'bits and pieces' of repair work, and the hiring and overseeing of boats to summer skin diving parties, who ploiter sleekly in their strictly rotated hundreds among the profusion of block-ships and other wrecks out in the Flow.

Robin, an affable, stubble-jowled man, spoke of 'better times' as he worked at a recalcitrant, salt-stained brass hinge with release oil. Of how, throughout the seventies, he and his brother had eight craftsmen working four nights overtime and a Saturday. Building, among other things, workboats for the Fishery Protection vessels, *Fingal*, *Polestar*, *Pharos*.

'That side of things is long dead,' he said stoically. 'The cost of timber, alone — larch, oak — can be around a quid per cubic foot, just for the shipping of it to Orkney. The funny thing is, there's a big upsurge nowadays in traditional work. Folks want the old wooden clinker-built job. But there aren't many left who know how to make them.'

A recently commissioned glass reinforced plastic job, was the first for twelve years. Repair work on Orkney's many small lobster boats, between the fallow months of June and July when lobsters and crabs cast off their shells, keeps their heads above water. It is an obvious though apt metaphor.

He released the brass hinge from the vice, and smiled. 'That's better now. You'd be daft to throw away *that* kind of quality nowadays.'

St. Margaret's Hope in South Ronaldsay — the largest and final island in the string — lodges in the throat of the bay. It is a Sunday morning in February. The two-tiered village is deserted, save for a street corner clutch of cronies who fall silent at my approach, then raise their arms in lazy salutation. I feel like the lonesome cowboy; the mysterious stranger in town, and couldn't be more wrong. For this is a place of 'ferry-loupers' and 'white settlers', as they're called by Orcadians — and rarely with malice.

Settlers like the casually met, Leicestershire-born, retired steeplejack, whose new roots already finger deeply down into the local loam. After working for twenty years at his trade in Australia, he and his wife, whilst on holiday in St. Margaret's Hope, fell in love with the place, bought and renovated a house, and were in the process of 'doing up' another. And 'sure, the locals were really helpful to us interlopers ... and still are,' he added keenly.

I've a liking for the place, myself. Ever since that still midsummer night of unbroken twilight, when my father's coastal rustbucket, pier-berthed, settled her ample belly on the sands of the outgoing tide.

There's Back Road: a gently curved brae of substantial dwellings, some of which have managed to retain the traditional Orkney stone roofing slabs. And Front Road (they don't muck about with twee street names here, thank God), its sea-fringed street, dirling to the sound of mash hammer and DIY saw. And The Bank of Scotland, 1873, douce, august and red of visage, glowering disdainfully seawards. There are three fine gable-ends nearby, complete with astragal windows. I also noticed the dreaded satellite dish (why are they circular? — the most commanding of shapes — and white). And I wish a certain corner dwelling in the vicinity of Cromarty Square, would re-think that chrome yellow paint scheme.

It seems likely that the name, St. Margaret's Hope — St. Margaret's Haven — is a reminder that a chapel, dedicated to St. Margaret of Scotland, queen of Malcolm Canmore and no connection with the ill-fated Margaret, Maid of Norway, graced this ancient haven. I see in my mind's eye, a chapel similar to that small, whitewashed Norman gem high in Edinburgh Castle rock.

Formerly a fishing centre of importance, St. Margaret's Hope once shared the commerce of Stromness and Kirkwall, and is, I'm glad to hear, enjoying a modest revival of its former sea trade.

South Ronaldsay is eight miles long by some three miles broad; is dipped deep in history, pre and recorded and, according to my schoolboy ruler, is $6\frac{1}{2}$ sea miles from the rocks of Brough Ness, to the car park and tourist viewpoint at Duncansby Head on mainland Scotland. It is a richly fertile place of low hills, the highest of which is Ward Hill, which is just short of 400 feet, and worth the climb for its views of the Pentland Firth, Hoy, Scapa Flow and the coast of Caithness. The high peaks of Northern Scotland can be seen on polished days.

Because of this close proximity to Scotland, it is possible that it was here that Orkneys first Christian missionaries landed. There are traces of some twelve or more ecclesiastical buildings, some of which are dedicated to such early Christian saints as St. Colm and St. Ninian.

There are frequent references to South Ronaldsay in the *Orkneyinga Saga*. It was in St. Margaret's Hope that King Hakon's fleet lay at anchor at the outset of his grand expedition to assert law and order in Scotland, and to demonstrate that he, the last great king of Norway, was determined that his island dominions were to be treated with respect.

The story goes that, whilst at anchor in St. Margaret's Hope, a total eclipse of the sun took place. Not a good omen in an age when such natural phenomena were regarded as signs of either good or evil. Undeterred, his vast fleet sailed one week later through the Pentland Firth and returned on the 29 October, a forlorn straggle of ships and men, due more to autumn storms and over ambition, than the so-called defeat at the Battle of Largs in 1263. Described by one historian as ' . . . this indecisive skirmish.'

The island today, is witness to gentler, though no less ancient manners and customs. Unique among which, is the Festival of the Horse, where boys with superbly crafted miniature ploughs — some of which are heirlooms — compete in a sand ploughing match. The girls, garish with sequins, ribbons and paper flowers, dress up as horses. Costumes and ploughs are then judged at St. Margaret's Hope. After which they boy ploughmen, sans 'horses', set off to the flat, damp sand of the beach at Sands o' Right, where they compete, under sharp-eyed adult judges, in getting the straightest and sweetest furrows. Originally (and to me, rightly) held at Easter, it is now held on the second Wednesday in August, to accommodate tourists.

One summer's evening in 1958, South Ronaldsay farmer, Ronald Simison, looking for those slabstones traditionally used in Orkney for fencing corner posts (strainers), noticed at a nearby mound that slabs revealed by recent heavy rains, ran vertically, not horizontally as is the nature of the rock strata about his policies. Curious, he soon discovered what appeared to be a man-made wall, and, spurred by this, began to scrape at the soil and turf with his fingers until he had exposed — within minutes — not only a section of wall, but also a cache of human bones and Stone Age objects: a polished stone ceremonial mace head, polished stone axe-heads and a knife, plus a finely-crafted and highly polished jet button.

Intrigued, he and his brother-in-law, Charlie Scott, delved deeper with spades, and, after a period of intensive digging exposed the top of a small entrance. The interior was dark. They could see nothing until one of them thrust the puny flame of his cigarette lighter into the tiny roofed chamber, the floor of which, was strewn with human skulls.

Further and more detailed examination of the site by professional archaeologists, showed that among this mass of human skulls and disarticulated human bones (16,000 in all: the remains of 342 individuals) were also those of animals. Prominent among which were the talons and carcasses of the white-tailed sea eagle: almost certainly the totem bird, or symbol of this particular Stone Age tribe. One only has to think of the tribal rituals of the American Indian of the not so distant past, and their totemic animals, to focus the imagination. Totems and the rituals surrounding them, were of great importance to tribal societies, for not only did they mark territories, but were regarded as ancestral to the living. The thing to which they would be united on death.

It soon became evident that the Tomb of the Eagles, as it was soon dubbed, was no ordinary burial chamber, but an ancestral charnel house for a tribe who, like certain present day Tibetans and the Zoroastrians of Persia and India, exposed their dead on platforms outside the tomb entrance. After which, they would ceremoniously place their bird-pecked bones in orderly rows in the shelved compartments of the tomb. It was clear, also, that animals such as calves and lambs were sacrificed, dismembered in the area and left both inside and outside the chamber, uncooked. The carapace of a crab was also found, along with limpet shells and over one thousand fish bones.

Not relishing the prospect of strangers invading his land, Ronald Simison and his wife, Morgan, loaned the tomb's artifacts to Tankerness House Museum in Kirkwall in 1978. Then later decided to set up their own museum in the conservatory of their farmhouse at Liddle Farm, South Ronaldsay. It was to be a *coup de théâtre* no subfusc museum committee could ever have conceived.

I was Morgan Simison's sole visitor that winter's day. She was about to hang out the washing, but changed gear with practised ease, to escort me wittily and imaginatively along the home-made showcases of skulls, axe-heads, beads and sea-eagle talons. I never dreamt I'd ever use that awful pop-museum term, 'Hands on Experience', but this was it personified, humanised and acceptable.

'Go on. Hold your grandfather's skull,' she said, lifting the old boy from the glass case. 'Now try this stone hammer.' I cradled my grandfather in the crook of my left arm and grasped the smooth stone. It was snug and rightly made. 'Beautifully balanced, eh? Now try this stone knife. Fits the hand well, doesn't it? Your grandfather wasn't stupid, you know.'

Her theories on the customs and day-to-day working routines of her subjects are, as you'll have gathered, refreshingly original and free from academic hoo-ha, and have that eternal we-womenfolk-have-seen-it-all-before, ring to them. Running her finger across the cranium of one Stone Age female, she said mischievously, 'That groove on the top of this poor souls head, was caused by having to carry heavy loads, while you lot were out hunting and scyving — as usual!'

The tomb is three-quarters-of-a-mile from the farm, and rests on the cliff's edge between Black Geo and North Taing.

Its claustrophobic entrance facing seawards. The trick is, to arrive there on your own, on a day of storms, unlock the tiny padlocked gate, and, gulping fetid air, crawl into the past. Time present, snapping at the soles of your feet.

Hugging the experience, I returned to the farm by the scenic cliff path, secure in the knowledge that sea- eagles breed still — albeit tenuously — along Scotland's western seaboard.

St. Mary's Church, Burwick, east of Isbister, is a pinched rectangle, grey harled and barnlike. Its sensible and sea-facing flank, windowless. Inside, pine pews close ranks and stiffen in the presence of the frivolously ornate pipe organ. Paraffin lamps hang from the ceiling.

Celtic in foundation, it is a place of legends. The most famous of which tells of how Magnus, pursued by enemies in Scotland, set out to cross the Pentland Firth in a coracle, unaware of the treacherous nature of those waters. In danger of drowning, he prayed that, if his life was spared, he would build a chapel to the Virgin at the spot where he should reach land. His prayers were immediately answered in the form of a sea monster (a dolphin, perhaps?) on whose back he reached the safety of Burwick, South Ronaldsay. As a constant reminder to Magnus of God's mercy (though no doubt to the consternation of the dolphin) his aquatic saviour was turned into stone. This miraculous metamorphosis, I'm told, can be seen at St. Mary's Church, is boat-shaped, measures some four feet by two feet wide, and bears two depressions in the centre resembling human footprints. Despite, or perhaps because of my familiarity with this hallowed spot, I've never found it. Is it still there? And if so, where?

There are no dramatic vistas. No tourist trails or grand sites of historical interest here at the bay. Some would label it dull — rundown, even. But for me it has that indefinable otherness. That spirit of place.

A friend who stayed in the area for some years, puts it better: 'My house faced the sea. There was a small hill at the back. Nothing grand, you know. But I miss that place still. I felt, well, contained there. Held,' she said, butting the heels of her cupped hands.

CHAPTER SIX
Hoy: the Dark Island

Hoy Hills are moor-dark and boggy. A parting gift from Highland gods. They say Orkney's shoal of flat, viridian islands were just as dour, before the ancient ones began to sweeten the face of the land. It must have been a gey sore wresting.

Hoy (HÁEY 'high island') is the second largest island in Orkney and the most dramatic, for Ward Hill and the Cuilags rule over all here. This most Highland of places boasts a variety of wild flowers, plants and indigenous trees such as rowan, aspen and hazel. Plus a richness of common and not so common lepidoptera with splendid names: *Hepialus fuscanebulosa* De Geer, *Noctua janthina* D & Schiff.

According to a report by the Nature Conservancy Council, a pair of golden eagles have been breeding successfully on Hoy since 1966, after an absence of over a century. Their diet consisting of fulmars and blue hares. Here, too, as one can imagine, are the wildland homes of buzzard, kestrel and hen harrier. Not forgetting the midge — that dipterous scourge of Highland holidays — on Orkney's rare, sticky and windless summer days.

Respectful souls will, I know, pay proper homage to the flora and fauna of this, or any other place. Recent reports in *The Orcadian* newspaper, however, tell of the disturbing summer season habit of visitors uprooting clumps of Orkney's vivid masses of sea pinks, in the mistaken belief that those hardy miracles will take root in tamed suburban soils.

The ferry crossing from the Bay of Houton to Lyness is short, speedy and vehicle packed, and skirts the islands of Cava, Rysa Little and Fara, on either side of Gutter Sound. The pier and its environs at Lyness are unpromising introductions to one of Orkneys most romantic and myth-soaked islands.

Lyness was an important and strategic military and naval base for two world wars: the concrete stumps and rusting reminders of which, still show, not only here but throughout the island. Constructed in haste on both occasions, the harbour area was refashioned, used for as long as was needed, then left by the Ministry of Defence, warts and all, with no attempt made to return the land to its former state. Farmers, I read, are still unable to plough certain areas of land due to buried concrete oil tanks and other suchlike hidden detritus.

Lyness Bay Visitor Centre goes some small way towards rectifying the dereliction and sad souvenirs of war. In the yard, a black and petrified long-range gun, its breech a starlings nest, points impotently towards Scapa Flow. An amphibious troop landing carrier, steam crane and highly-beezed khaki-green field gun, crouch in the shadow of the thirty five ton, twelve foot high propellor and shaft of the ill-fated cruiser *Hampshire* which was lifted by a German salvage ship in 1985.

The visitor centre, proper, oozes bittersweet essences of nostalgia. Gap-toothed and Brylcreemed matlos with 'hello mum' grins, beam out from Box Brownie snaps. And youngsters, weaned on 'smart weapons' and the tomato sauce wounds of video wars, cock and fire Bren and Lanchester sub-machine guns, pull on gas masks, don tin hats and fumble with the pins of dead grenades, with more than a little help from dad.

There's also a moving display of photographs and relief maps relating to the sinking of the *Royal Oak*, the oil from which, still seeps in rainbow hues from her bunkers after fifty years. There are barnacle encrusted binnacles and similarly salt-pickled memorabilia. And sailors faded cap bands with nostalgic names: *Jade, Raleigh, Dragon, Beagle, Brazen, Bridgewater.*

As you leave Lyness, take the Rackwick leg of the B9047, skirting the naval cemetery to your left. Continue for approximately four miles, and brake above the moor-girt grave next to Water of Hoy. The roadside legends says it all:

'Betty Corrigall was a girl who lived at Lyness during the last century. She was in love with a sailor, but the sailor left Hoy on a ship and never returned. Upon realizing she was pregnant by him she was so ashamed she tried to drown herself. Neighbours pulled her out, then she hanged herself in the byre.

At that time, suicide was considered a sin and so she could not be buried in consecrated ground. The Lairds of Hoy and Melsetter refused her burial on their estates and, as a result, she was buried on the parish border.

The grave was rediscovered in the early 1930s by peat cutters, and in 1949 an American minister, the Rev. Kenwood Bryant on a visit to Hoy, made a wooden cross for the grave and surrounded it with a picket fence. He asked Mr Harry Berry, Customs and Excise Officer for Hoy, if he would make a gravestone and Mr Berry promised to do this when he had the time. Mr Berry retired in 1976, and it was then that he finally found some spare time to make the headstone. He wrote to the Rev. Bryant in the USA informing him that he would now keep his promise, to which he received the reply — "Some people cannot keep a promise after 27 minutes, let alone 27 years!"

The land around the grave is a peat bog and a heavy stone would require a deep foundation. Betty Corrigall's grave had been disturbed twice in previous years so Mr Berry decided he would make the headstone from fibreglass, to avoid disturbing the grave again. As it was not known if there had been a burial service at the time of her death, Mr Berry and two friends stood around the grave one evening in 1976 and performed a short burial service.'

If you think that tale of intolerance is unique to the nineteenth century, then think on. For it's a sobering thought that such as Betty Corrigall were labelled *moral defectives*, antisocial in conduct, and were often incarcerated for life by their 'moral superiors' in institutions for the insane and mentally handicapped, well into the twentieth century.

If it were possible (God forbid!) to find oneself dumped, then, after having the blindfold removed, asked to locate this place, I'd make a stab at Caithness, or somewhere thereabouts. For this is a brooding pass between the mist-scalped hump of Ward Hill and the high rocky outcrop of Dwarfie Hammars. And as far removed from the sky-washed horizontals of Orkney as the Malvern's are from Suilven. A perfect setting for Hoys only, though most enigmatic chambered tomb.

The Dwarfie Stane squats on a rise overlooking the moor, one third of a mile from the car park. For long the focus of legend and superstition, the stone is a rock-cut tomb, some ten paces long by five, broad, tapering from six feet to two feet. There are extremely small side cells within the short, low chamber. A large blocking stone lies at the entrance. What makes this tomb unique among Orkneys many ancient tombs, is that it has been hollowed out from the natural sandstone rock by human hands, using the most primitive of stone tools, the marks of which, can be seen on the roof of the south cell. Similar in concept to rock-cut tombs in the Mediterranean megalithic tradition, it is more than likely of local inspiration. Earlier theories claim that it was a hermits cells with two bed-places for people of an unusually short stature — hence its name. That it was the tomb of two mortals, laid to rest in the foetal position, seems more than likely.

There were, of course, those who swore it was the residence of the local troll. Stuff and nonsense! Mind you, I wouldn't cross that moor, alone, on a moonlit night for all the Highland Park in Kirkwall.

It comes as no surprise that the brooding nature of this place has spawned the most plausible tales of the supernatural. Ernest W. Marwick in his fascinating and definitive *Folklore of Orkney and Shetland*, tells of a Mr W.E. Turner of Luton, Bedfordshire, who spent nearly two years in Hoy during the Second World War, and who wrote to him to a describe ' ... a never-to-be forgotten experience', thus:

'One stormy day in winter I was walking or struggling along the cliff top at Tor Ness. The wind was high and howled about, low-lying, swirling clouds part-enveloped the land in misty rain. At times the pressure was so great that I was forced to bend and clutch at the heather to retain a footing. On one such occasion on looking up I was amazed to see that I had the company of what appeared to be a dozen or more "wild men" dancing about, to and fro.

These creature were small in stature, but they did not have long noses nor did they appear kindly in demeanour. They possessed round faces, sallow in complexion with long, dark bedraggled hair. As they danced about, seeming to throw themselves over the cliff edge, I felt that I was a witness to some ritual dance of a tribe of primitive men. It is difficult to describe in a few words my feelings at this juncture or my bewilderment. The whole sequence could have lasted about three minutes until I was able to leave the cliff edge.'

There are other tales of fairy rings, giants, women who peddled fine weather and fair winds to sailors, and one-eyed sea monsters, in whose red raw flesh, were yellow veins, through which pulsed blood as black as tar.

I scan Rackwick determined to ban those down-at-heel adjectives: haunting, desolate, isolated, incomparable, only to hear myself declaim those self-same purplish nonsenses to an indifference of ruined crofts and gulls. For the place is indeed all of those things, with a dash of stunning stirred in to enrich the broth.

It sits in a hollow facing the Atlantic; the narrow Glens of Kinnaird at its back. A thriving place of fishermen and spinners and knitters of wool, the land lies derelict. There was a wee school here, but that, too, closed in 1954 when its remaining pupils — two brothers — were drowned when their home-made raft overturned in the South Burn, where it opens to the sea. Their parents left soon after, and never returned.

Garry Hogg, in his book *The Far-Flung Isles*, recalls visiting what was left of their home:

> 'Through the shadowed windows we looked in and saw a horsehair chair with three odd child's shoes strewn on it, some fragments of crumbling peat in a fire-place red with rust, an empty lemonade bottle on a shelf, a broken tumbler in a corner, and a single woollen glove dangling over a string stretched beneath the mantelpiece where it had hung to dry last time there had been burning peat in the hearth.'

And George Mackay Brown in the introduction to his poem cycle, *Fishermen with Ploughs*, writes:

> 'The valley is drained of its people. The Rackwick croft ruins are strewn with syrup tins, medicine bottles, bicycle frames, tattered novels, portraits of Queen Victoria.'

Though fewer in number, the ruins are there still, butt-end to the sea. There's a back-packer's hostel, the acceptable face of car parks, and an unobtrusive toilet. The bay rings to the sounds of a transitory and anxious race, here for the day. Their city wounds bathed by the sounds and silences of this place of shadows, somewhere at the world's end.

Composer, Peter Maxwell Davies, came to Orkney one June during the annual and internationally renowned St. Magnus Festival, fell in love with the place, found himself a near derelict croft on an exposed Rackwick hillside and, inspired by sea-sounds and the poetry of George Mackay Brown, began to compose what I've come to regard as the most gripping chamber and orchestral music of the late twentieth century. I particularly like his setting for soprano and guitar of two Mackay Brown poems, *The Drowning Brothers* (based on the tragic incident I touched on previously), and *Dead Fires*, a haunting evocation of a ruined Rackwich croft. His *Hymn to St. Magnus*, based on the twelfth century original from St. Magnus Cathedral, is a powerful eulogy of the virtues and martyrdom of the Saint. As is his setting of Mackay Brown's *From Stone to Thorn*, in which the ritual of the Stations of the Cross is paralleled with the older ritual of agriculture. His *Symphony* (named just that) had its origins in 1973 in an unperformed, long, single orchestral movement previously called *Black Pentecost*, from the already mentioned *Dead Fires*. Other movements followed until the work outgrew its original form. There are other works, too numerous to mention here. Hear him!

His mist-skeined head pokes above the horizon, and I have second, darker thoughts, about this picture postcard cliché: this so-called Old Man of Hoy, I'd seen so often at a distance, from the decks of ships. I'm unprepared for the full-frontal, close-up and unexpurgated version. That he towers *above* what are in themselves lip-biting cliffs, adds to the drama. He really *is* far too big for his sea-thrashed boots.

I retreat crabwise from the cliff's edge and the rackety spume below and beyond, and marvel at the divine arrogance that prompted Chris Bonnington to sclim the old boys east face in 1966, and Hamish McInnes to make his television free ascent, sans pitons, the year after.

Hoy and its hills are such dominant characters among Orkney's low, green sprinklings, that one is apt to forget that the place is divided into two unequal parts: Hoy (the larger by far) and Walls. Linked in recent times by a road across the narrow channel between North Bay and Aith Hope.

Here, too, are Martello towers. Those dour reminders of the Napoleonic wars. Dumb guardians at the mouth of Longhope, at the head of which stands the mansion house of Melsetter (pronounced mel'ster), former house of the Moodie family: Jacobite sympathisers and overlords for two centuries of an estate which include the islands of Hoy, Walls, Rysa Little and Fara. Bought and renovated by a wealthy English leather manufacturer at the turn of the century, it is an unlikely home for those unfussy and well-made items of furniture we associate with the Arts and Crafts Movement. The architect in overall charge of the extension and renovation, was one of William Morris's acolytes who, upholding that movement's philosophy of simplicity wedded to quality, engaged some of Orkney's finest craftsmen to make chairs, tables and sideboards to the designs of such artistic luminaries as Ford Maddox Brown, and Dante Gabriel Rossetti. The estate was divided and up for grabs in the twenties. The house was requisitioned during both world wars to house the top brass of the admiralty.

You either love or hate that other local landmark, 'The Garrison'. I love it ... well, sort of. Its completely out of context, fumbling, black and white mock Art Deco facade makes me smile. For it was in garrison theatres like this, throughout Britain, that such stars of radio and film as Gracie Fields, George Formby, Arthur Askey and Old Mother Riley, distributed their gifts of song and laughter. Dispelling, if only for a moment, the boredom of the home-posting they called Orkney.

Longhope Lifeboat Station is known throughout the country. The men who have manned it, famed for their seamanship and selfless acts of courage. Like coxswain Dan Kirkpatrick and his crew, who, at great risk to themselves, rescued the crew of the trawler, *Strathcoe*, which had gone aground beneath the Hoy cliffs.

There was tragedy and human loss, too, that night of March 1969, when the Longhope lifeboat, *TGB* went out in a skreever of a force nine sou'-easterly, in answer to a Mayday call from the Liberian cargo ship *SS. Irene*, in difficulties off Halcro Head. Next day the lifeboat was found upturned off the coast of Walls, not far from the station. Her crew of eight, dead. *SS. Irene* grounded, and her crew were subsequently rescued by breeches-buoy. The coxswain and second coxswain had their two sons with them that night. They were buried in Longhope cemetery.

The people in the peedie township of Brims will honour their memory, for as long as there are those who voluntarily, and with full knowledge of the sea's caprisciousness, go to the aid of those who go down to the sea in ships.

CHAPTER SEVEN

Shapinsay, Gairsay, Rousay, Eynhallow, Egilsay, Wyre, Eday, Sanday, Stronsay, Westray, Papa Westray, North Ronaldsay

'Take the wheel and head for that point of land to starboard,' he said, as we puttered out of Kirkwall harbour in his converted ship's lifeboat. It was the perfect way for a romantic and over-the-hill Soothlan to return to a place he'd last set foot on thirty years ago.

So why in the name of Thorarin Bag-Nose did the damned engine start to overheat? We'd greased the prop-shaft, checked the life jackets, pumped the bilges and other things familiar to those who muck about in boats. Why now, just as I was thrilling to the sea's unpredictable grip on the rudder? We bunged three gallons of fresh water into the hissing engine, and limped back (yes, that's the clichè) into harbour. No intertwined gold torque on Nordic bicepts. Just Garson Beard-Soaked, queuing for the 5-45 shop assistants bus back to Stromness.

I made the short sea crossing eventually, some five years later, on a stouter and more dependable, though duller craft.

Shapinsay is the nearest of the inner North Isles to Kirkwall, and is popular with day trippers. Four miles long by two miles broad, it is flat, featureless and lushly cultivated. On maps it resembles a bird in flight: its beak at Haco's Ness, wing-tip at Ness of Ork, tail feathers stretching from The Galt, to Twi Ness. There are no breath-stopping views, but the drive to The Hillock, along what must surely be one of Orkney's straightest secondary roads, is a joy.

The fertility of the land is due largely to the vision of one, Major Balfour, who introduced modern farming methods to Shapinsay as long ago as the late eighteenth century. And who, by all accounts, behaved in a civil fashion towards his estate workers.

According to contemporary records, Balfour appears to have brought a touch of Southern Counties England, to what was then a waste land, inhabited by gaunt and threadbare peasants, made indifferent by despair. As full-time resident of his estate, it was possible, also, for him to monitor the moods and pace of his workers, and to reward or punish as he saw fit.

His heir, Colonel David Balfour, bought more lands with the fortune he'd amassed in India; became Member of Parliament for Orkney and Shetland in 1790, and began to build Balfour Castle, the islands over-the-top and incongruous showpiece. Designed by David Bryce between 1846 and 1850, it is a model of all that adjectival style stands for: castellated, turreted, crow-stepped and corbelled. There are capacious rooms to match, filled with appropriately grand furniture and artifacts. A fine walled garden and dense stands of sinuous trees complete the scene.

Shapinsay's other claim to fame is more indirect and less known. It was from here that local lad, William Irvine left the sea to emigrate to New York in the eighteenth century, where he 'took to trade'. It was to be a fruitful move in more ways than one, for his wife gave birth to eleven bairns, the youngest of which was born in 1783, and christened Washington, after the President. He studied law, but was sent to Europe because of delicate health. Just how delicate, we don't know. Although he did manage to visit all the great capitals of Europe. Admitted to the bar after his foreign travels, he turned to essay and short story writing under the pseudonym, 'Geoffrey Crayon', after the collapse of his father's business, and produced a great number of stylishly written works; two of which — *Rip Van Winkle*, and *The Legend of Sleepy Hollow* — were to become popular classics. He was appointed Ambassador to Spain in 1842, and died in 1859.

Unlike the island of Hoy, it's difficult to associate this green and pleasant place with the folklore or Orkney. But there was, by all accounts, a fairy doctor in Shapinsay: specialists in curing such things as convulsions, and the so-called 'wasting' diseases caused by supernatural beings. One, Duncan J. Robertson heard an account of someone having witnessed one such fairy doctor waving his arms, and dancing with the little folk one night on a hilltop. The fairies were invisible to the eye witness. I think the good doctor had drank deeply and well of the golden potion.

The only large island among Orkney's green scatter not mentioned in the Norse Sagas, there are nevertheless, many unexcavated prehistoric mounds, and other reminders of Shapinsay past. Like the megalithic stump, Mör Steen, or Moora Stone, a mile south-east of Ward Hill, approximately two hundred yards north of Cot-on-Hill farm. And the so-called Black Stone of Odin, or Odin's Stone, situated on the north shore on the edge of Veantro Bay. There are fine farm dwellings, too. And a lovely mill above the bay at Elwick. Plus the ubiquitous craft shops and tearooms.

Don't leave the island without buying either a whole, or generous wedge of hand-made Shapinsay cheese. For it's a *real* Orkney cheese: pale, moist, subtle of flavour and slightly salty, with that distinctive hint of buttermilk. So common once in my youth, though now sadly something of a gourmet item, I'm thankful that there are a few, still, who continue the tradition, not only in Shapinsay, but in the other isles and parishes of Orkney.

GAIRSAY

Gairsay is dome-shaped, and lies south of Gairsay Sound and the island of Wyre. It is a barren place, best known historically as the winter retreat of Svein Asleifarson, last of the hardman Vikings, and thorn in the flesh of the Earls. A man who lived to fight, and who sought the least opportunity to do so, he was killed in 1171, whilst attempting to conquer Dublin.

It is believed the remains of his great drinking hall — skala — where he thought nothing of entertaining his eighty armed warriors at a sitting, lies beneath Langskaill House, built in the seventeenth century for Sir William Craigie and his wife.

Unlike the Victorian pomposity of Shapinsay Castle, Langskaill House, though mostly derelict, is, as Jim Crumley's introductory poem says '... Orkney all the way through'. Its great simplicity enhanced by the orantely carved archway scroll, armorial panel, and the we-mean-business gun-loops of the gateway, originally the only means of access to the house.

The old harvest customs of this small land lingered well into the twenties. Ernest W. Marwick tells of one, relating to the harvest bannock which was made from the last sheaf to be cut, in the belief that the corn spirit dwelt within. A bizarre sequence of events followed when the lad who carted the final load of sheaves into the yard had his trousers forcibly removed by his mates, who then proceeded to scrub his bare backside with the rough butt-end of the sheaf. Then, as if that weren't pain enough, the man of the house would hand the poor soul a bannock baked by his wife, then told to run, his pursuers baying at his heels. If he managed to outrun them, he would sit and eat his bannock in peace. If not, they would grab it from his hand. The one who, in the scramble, managed to seize the largest piece of bannock, claimed himself victor.

The ancient and solemn custom may have deteriorated by then into little more that youthful devilment, but I regret its passing. It beats boy-racing in stolen cars.

ROUSAY

It's about time we/they stopped referring to Rousay as 'the Egypt of the North'. I understand why, of course. The island is richly endowed with sites of major archaeological interest: but Egypt? surely not, in this place of mists and mosses and steps-and-stairs braes sloping towards the sly tide-rips of Rousay Sound.

Serious lovers of things Orcadian will want to spend some time here, and are advised to consult Kirkwall or Stromness's

B&B oracles beforehand — especially during the tourist-turgid months of June, July and August.

For those less inclined to explore the island in depth, or those unable to tramp heather hills, I'd recommend the Westness Walk to Midhowe Cairn and Broch. (Again, day-trippers, consult the oracles). Though studded with finger posts and waymarkers — those inescapable, sticky-uppy, walk-this-way nonsenses which increasingly desecrate the footpaths, woodlands, beaches and moors of Britain — Rousay's wear a discreet and acceptable face. Spawned by Orkney Islands Council in collaboration with Scottish Conservation Projects and the Countryside Commission, the Walk opened to the public in 1987, and has been a great success with visitors ever since. It's easy to understand why, for only the densest of souls would fail to respond to the views across Eynhallow Sound. That apart, the walk, too, is a pleasant jaunt, even on those days when sea mists curl in from the Atlantic, or when gales cut through the mouth of Eynhallow Sound.

Midhowe Chambered Cairn lies close to the shore, between Fishing Geo and Geo of Skaill. It is enclosed within a large hangar-like structure to protect it from the elements: such is its importance, archaeologically. The interior can be viewed at ground-level, and from overhead gantries. Corridor-like, and immense with it, at 76ft long by 7ft wide, it is a fine example of a stalled cairn, divided into twenty-four burial compartments, twelve-a-side, by a series of upright stone slabs. Should you find my descriptive powers lacking, simply imagine something resembling a large cow byre. Decorative herring-bone patterns in edge stones can be seen on the cairn's outer east face, and add to the impression that this must have a been a chamber of some importance.

On excavation, the undisturbed and carefully placed remains of seventeen adults, six adolescents and two children were found along the east side of the chamber. There were little or no artifacts other than pottery shards, limpet shells, and the bones of birds and farm animals.

Nearby Midhowe Broch, like the Broch of Gurness, Mainland, is a squat, circular ruin whose original 'cooling tower' structure was demolished over the years for dykes and sheep fanks, and other peaceful uses. Though lacking the loftily-preserved presence of the great Broch of Mousa in Shetland, it is an impressive ruin perched on the cliff promontory.

A fair quantity of artefacts were found in and around the broch during excavation, many of which were of Roman origin, and probably trading (or loot) gifts from Southern parts, as the northernmost isles were more than the great Roman legions, even, could tackle.

Viking graves, too, are in abundance in this wondrous isle. And none more remarkable than the one discovered in the sixties by a local farmer who, on spading a pit for a dead cow, came across the skeletal remains of a lass and her newborn bairn, plus a wealth of grave gifts, among which was the by now priceless, so-called *Westness Brooch*: a thing of great and simple beauty, chased with interlaced linear patterns, and the stylized heads of fiercely-beaked birds.

Moa Ness promontory, just off the Westness Walk, was an important burial site for Pict and Viking alike. Some Viking graves, contrary to the shallow, made-to-measure scrapings of the Pict, were oval-shaped and stashed with the tools and implements of the dead man's trade. Viking boat graves were not uncommon in the ninth century, hereabouts, within which the deceased was laid amidships in his Norse yole (a clinker-built boat, sharp at stem and stern), tools and weapons to hand.

I often think how much more dignified those methods of burial among both, the ancient ones and their Norse successors must have been, compared to our hasty, late twentieth century despatchings, where the grave's clay, even, is masked by carpets of plastic grass, and Bach's Jesu, Joy of Man's Desiring comes canned, in souless crematoria.

Waymarked routes apart, there's nowt to beat the twelve mile stroll of the island's circumference, from pier-to-pier. Granted, it's a road walk — something I'd avoid normally — but what a road! Especially on one of those late winter days when the air and sky are Swiss-like. Not that you have to stick to the road, for there are endless things of interest to divert the walker, en-route; such as the crannog (an artificial Stone Age island, often fortified and used as a refuge) on the Loch of Wasbister. And the buttressed ruins of the Post Reformation Church of St. Mary's, adjacent to the foundations of the square medieval stone tower known as The Wirk. The excavated Norse farmstead close to the Knowe of Swanda, with longhouses, halls and byres, is worth a visit.

Super-fit pilgrims will want to top the walking day with a quick pad to the summit of High Brae of Camps. The views are, well, breathtaking.

And as one of Maurice Walsh's enigmatic, tweed-clad, pipe-smoking heroes might have said to passer-by and friend alike: 'God bless the day!'

EYNHALLOW

The tiny uninhabited green isle of Eynhallow (Hildaland) lies halfway between Rousay and Mainland: tormented by the tide roosts of Eynhallow Sound.

Known to Orcadians as 'the Isle', it was once called the Holy Isle; for a monastery stood there more than eight centuries ago, to which chieftains sent their sons to be educated.

It is a place of legends; fed, I imagine, by its inaccessibility. They called it 'the Vanishing Isle,' not so long ago. But then, such mirages were not uncommon in northern parts. Eynhallow, though, was something else, for the place belonged to 'the sea-folk'. And the story goes that, if a Rousay man took a knife, or similar piece of steel in both hands (for trows fear cold steel more than anything) and, launching his boat, braved the roosts, never for a moment taking his eyes off the island, steel, firmly gripped until he came ashore, he would have captured the island from the trows, and the place would be his for all time.

Many a Rousay man, they say, attempted it, and many drowned in the roost. One made it, though. Which is why, ever since that day, Eynhallow has been regarded by the people of Rousay as belonging to them.

The sea-folk lurk and sulk there yet, their rage embodied in the frenzied white waters.

EGILSAY

Cousins, Hakon Paulsson and Magnus Erlendsson ruled Orkney jointly. It was an uneasy arrangement between two incompatible personalities. Hakon, wild in youth, bold and unscrupulous in manhood. Popular with his men. A chieftain with an eye ever swivelled for the main chance. Magnus, quiet and dreamy — or so we are led to believe. A sixteenth century, polychromed altarpiece from Andenes, Nordland, show him as a foppish and powdered, pot-bellied, almost Wildean figure, with a rosebud mouth and cascades of blonde, shoulder-length hair. A far cry from the adjacent and cocky manliness of St Olav; and an even further cry from those keen-jawed, Dan Dare icons we have come to regard as saints and warriors Nordic.

An account in the Orkneyinga Saga, tells how Magnus refused to fight at the battle of Anglesey Sound, whilst on board King Magnus Bareleg's of Norway's ship, but slipped ashore at the first opportunity, under cover of darkness, then proceeded northwards to seek refuge with King Malcolm and a bishop in Wales. After King Magnus Barelegs was dead, he returned to Orkney to claim his share in the earldom. Cousin Hakon — understandably — was not amused.

Magnus's personality wasn't all sweetness and light, for, after his Scottish sojourn, he appears to have overcome his reluctance to fight, as both cousins did battle with their foes, together. To the extent, even, of burning a Shetland man's house above his head.

Hugh Marwick, writer, sums it up well: 'It is very difficult to discern his real personality through the mists of hagiological panegyric that obscure his record.'

It was to prove an uneasy and short-lived alliance. A festering peace which came to a head in the island of Egilsay during Easter week of 16th April 1116.

A conference was arranged between them, from which it was assumed — by Magnus at any rate — all differences between them would be settled amicably and finally. Hakon arrived with eight ships, not two, which each had agreed upon. Magnus was seized and, begging for his life, was ready even to accept being maimed, blinded and imprisoned. Hakon supported this request, but his followers insisted that one or the other had to die. For clearly, the islands were too small to hold them both.

Hakon then ordered his standard-bearer, Ofeig, to carry out the execution, but he refused. The job — for such it was — was given to his cook, Lifolf, who, weeping loudly, was told by Magnus not to be afraid, and that the man who gave him his orders was a greater sinner than he.

Magnus took off his tunic and gifted it to Lifolf, according to the ancient customs and laws, then knelt for a moment in prayer.

'Stand in front of me and strike me hard on the head. It's not fitting for a chieftain to be beheaded like a thief,' he said, entreating the poor man to 'take heart.'

He crossed himself, and bent to receive the axe's blow on the left side of his skull.

Hakon ruled alone, after the murder of his cousin, and journeyed to Rome, where he received absolution from the Pope for his crime. And ruled thereafter, not only fairly, but well.

The site of his execution was miraculously transformed from a place '... rocky and overgrown with moss,' into a green field. A lumpish cenotaph stands on the spot. Oystercatchers and terns protest at the intrusion of their wind-thrashed privacy. Lacquered marsh marigolds sip from spongy hollows, and daisies star the workaday fields.

Did he, I wonder, face east as Lifolf stood by with the axe? Did he see what I saw that Easter's day, some eight hundred years after? The blue-green seas of Westray Firth, and the cloud-chased skies above Eday.

Egilsay is flat and looks like a prehistoric flint scraper on the OS map. It is approximately three miles long, inhabited, and dominated by the round-towered church of St Magnus, which resembles a grain silo from afar. A bloated dead seal lies above the tideline. Rusting cars and obsolete farm machinery form a dishevelled guard of honour above the pier head. The place wears an honest, lived-in face. There are no waymarkers.

Built by Norse settlers in the twelfth century, St Magnus' Church is the only example of a round-towered church in Scotland; although similar round-towered churches exist in Ireland, East Anglia and Germany. Dedicated to Magnus Erlendsson, it is possible that it stands on the site of an earlier church in which Magnus prayed before his death. Built from local stone, and a masterpiece of the masons craft, it consists of a rectangular nave, some nine paces long by five broad, with a square-ended barrel-vaulted chancel; above which is a small room known as the grief house, from the Old Norse *Grio*, meaning sanctuary. The tower would have been taller and conically capped, and would have served as a sanctuary-consisting of some four to five storeys-against peripatetic yobbos. Clever use has been made of the tower windows, some of which face each quarter of the compass. But it's the lively stonework surrounding the arched doorway and arrowslit windows which, for me, make the place that bit special. The rough wooing of plane and edge, and the boldly-hewn voussoirs like stylized rays of the sun.

WYRE

Wyre is smaller, though similar in outline to neighbouring Egilsay, and gets its name from the Old Norse, *vigr*, meaning spearhead, which both those islands resemble in plan.

Topographical charms apart, the star attraction of Wyre is Cubbie Roo's Castle: the earliest stone-built castle in Scotland, famed in recent years more for its original and legendary resident, than for its thick-skinned defensive merits. Built in the twelfth century by the Norse chieftain Kolbein Hruga, I am struck by how small and vulnerable it looks, compared to other defensive structures in Britain. But, according to the Hakon Saga, when it was besieged in 1231, it proved to be so impregnable that negotiations for a truce were speedily set in motion. I imagine though, that Hruga's considerable presence and reputation had some bearing on the decision; for huge he was, if his nickname Hruga ('heap') is anything to go by. A powerful and influential chieftain in every respect. So-much-so, that his name has been linked with Orkney's many giant stories — hence Cubie Roo, that perpetually petulant giant whose main occupation seems to have been that of hurling boulders at similarly petulant, boulder-hurling giants on other islands. There are many such blocks of stone which bear his name, notable among which, is the roughly cubical block known as the Finger Steen, on Rousay's shore which, it is claimed, Cubbie flung from Fitty Hill in Westray at his enemy in Kearfea in Rousay, but it fell short.

He also had a mania for bridge, or causeway building between islands. An extra-mural pursuit which never seemed to go right for poor old Cubbie, for on each occasion, the headband supporting his massive basket of stones would snap, and the piles of boulders became the mounds and skerries we see to this day.

Nearby St Mary's Chapel was built in the twelfth century to serve the Christian Norse family at the Hall of Bu (a farm), the name of which lingers in the present farm Bu of Wyre. The rectangular nave and square chanel are typical of their kind. Traces of the original plaster rendering — like that of Orphir Round Church — can be seen on the inside walls.

It was at the Bu that the poet Edwin Muir spent that childhood which he recalls with enviable lucidity in *An Autobiography*. A childhood where '... the crevices in stone walls were filled with secrets; a slab of hard cement on the wall of the house had a special meaning. Mud after rain was delicious, and I was charmed by everything that flew from the humble bee to the Willie Longlegs. At that stage the novelty of seeing a creature fly outweighs everything else.'

EDAY, SANDAY, STRONSAY

The *St Suniva* is a warrior for the working day. Her open deck stacked skilfully with fish boxes, a skipful of briquettes, pallets of yoghurt and chocolate mousse, destined for some tiny North Isles shop, sheets of corrugated roofing, fencing stabs, a clarty jeep, polished cars. An excitable man with a flap-over hairstyle, pans his whirring retirement present over the bustling stage, with its well-rehearsed cast of boiler-suited deckhands. Stilted Australian accents seep from the television set in the uptop lounge, where a pallid-faced boy picks his nose as he gawps unseeingly at the grainy, raw-hued images. Those regulars who have seen it all before, take tea and biscuits below decks in the spartan cafeteria.

It's a seven, to eight-hour-long round trip from Kirkwall to Eday, Sanday and Stronsay. And a day of hard graft for crew and skipper, alike. For there are no cushy ro-ro piers in these parts where vessels are literally inched into harbour, and cargoes are derrick-slung onto the quayside.

Muckle Green Holm off the tail-end of Eday, looks like a semi-submerged flute. Binoculars say, a string of caves along the east face, you over imaginative fool!

Eday is between seven to eight miles in length: a long dark ridge, high in the north and south and wasp-waisted amidships, from which isthmus — or 'aith' — it gets its name, Eday, or aith island.

It was famed once throughout Orkney and Scotland for the quality of its peats, which were exported to such peatless islands as Sanday and North Ronaldsay. Scotlands whisky distillers, too, prized the Eday peats above others, for the distinctive flavour it imparted to the Water of Life.

Today the island is popular with birdwatchers who salivate at the sight of awthing from the curlew-like whimbrel, to the dapper and black-bibbed ringed plover. There's B&B accommodation, a co-op shop, private and self-hire cars, plus the ubiquitous craftpersons.

There's a fine Maes Howe-type mound at the north end on Vinquoy Hill. To get there, follow the minor road which skirts Mill Loch. It's an easy and pleasant daunder to the cairn, and the views are just, well, dandy.

The nearby Stone of Setter is surely the most dramatic of Orkneys many standing stones. Sculpted by time it stands over fifteen feet-high, and bears an uneasy resemblance to the wrist and fingers of the human hand. Though no longer visible, it is said that the monolith carried the Latin inscription: *Andreas Matheson hucusque fugit a Veneficiis Ducis Weller 1755* (Andrew Matheson fled here from the sorcerer Captain Weller in 1755). Matheson, a ship's surgeon, it seems, was convinced his skipper had evil magic powers which were getting to him, hence his escape to Eday.

Carrick House, on the shore of Bay of Carrick overlooking Calf Sound, was built in the seventeenth century by John Stewart; prospective heir to the Earldom of Orkney, and younger son of the hugely loathed, Earl Robert Stewart. Architecturally undistinguished, it is better known for the part it played in the capture of pirate John Gow, by a later owner, James Fea, after Gow's ship foundered on the Calf of Eday. The bell from Gow's ship, *Revenge*, is preserved at the house.

It's a dramatic and wild and beautiful part, the north end. Stand on the point of Red Head beyond Otters Pool on a fierce day, the tides ramstamming through the narrows of Calf Sound, and you'll get my drift. There are evocative names to match: West Lesses, East Lesses. West Toe, East Toe. Little Noup Head and The Auks. And on the Calf of Eday: Lashy Taing, Goreys Saddle, Grotties Geo. The Knee.

The crew of the *St Suniva* off-load the fencing stabs, the cartons of chocolate mousse, the bright coils of barbed wire. Camcorder Man pans unsteadily across hold and pier, and the pallid-faced boy shoulders his immense pink and purple rucksack, and limps off into the drizzle.

A fat seal lolls on a nearby rocky outcrop, then floats off insouciantly as the swiftly rising tides swirl about his head.

In plan, Sanday resembles a discarded rag doll. Some say it looks like a lobster with its tail dipped in North Ronaldsay Sound, its head jammed between the Sounds of Spurness, Eday and Sanday. Writer, Hugh Marwick summed it up better when he referred to it as being 'all legs and arms'. Some sixteen miles-long, it is the flattest of the North Isles, famed for its spectacular sandy bays (hence the name 'Sand Island'), its rich pastures, the high quality of its beef cattle, and the successful co-operative of knitters, who hail from Sanday and the islands of Eday, North Ronaldsay and Stronsay. There are shops, schools, a small electronics firm, an hotel and guesthouse, plus a nine-hole golf course on Plain of Fidge, just off the B9069.

As I said, the place is flat. So-much-so that, from the air it looks as if it might sink into the sea at any moment. A great deal of the island, in fact, is so little above sea-level that in days of poor visibility, more ships have foundered among its cliffs and nesses than on any other Orkney Island. It is tempting to think that, whilst the islanders in the past would have undoubtedly done everything in their power to save the lives of shipwrecked seamen, their stranded vessels must have been something of a blessing in terms of fuel and goodies, on an island with no peats and precious few luxuries.

Birdwatching, beachcombing and the liquid pleasures of the tenth tee apart, there are sites of archaeological interest in this isle of many nesses. The most impressive of which is Quoyness Chambered Cairn on the tidal island of Elsness. A fine structure this, in the Maes Howe tradition, with its dauntingly impressive entrance and inner chamber. A similar, though sadly, ruined cairn known as Augmund Howe, lies close by to the south, surrounded by eleven smaller bronze-age burial mounds. Another nest of small cairns can be found on the point of Tofts Ness to the north.

Lighthouse buffs will want to see Start Point Lighthouse which stands on the extreme east of the island between Tobacco Rock and Lang Ware Taing. Start Point is a tidal island and can be reached at low tide, on foot. The light, like most of Britain's beacons, has been fully automatic since 1962.

The weel-to-do who held estates in Sanday, are too numerous to write about at length in this wee sketch, but the names Elpinstone, Stewart, Groat, Scalley and Traill figure in denser and more detailed historical accounts of the island. The surname, Sinclair, which originated in France from St Clare, in the fourteenth century, and is the most common surname in Orkney, is very much alive, and well, and living today in this amorphous and enchanted isle.

It's a tricky one, Stronsay. A display of finely-tuned navigational skills as the *St Suniva* inches towards the pier at Papa Sound. This skipper — as we used to say in my shipyard years — could turn her about on a tanner.

I'm surprised to see so many large and sophisticated two-storeyed dwellings strung beyond the pier-head, some of which are models of indigenous Orcadian architecture. And learn later that the village of Whitehall was home to the herring fishers and their families during the great herring boom in the nineteenth century, when as many as 1,500 seasonal female gutters and packers worked in the curing sheds around the village and on the tiny island of Papa Stronsay across the sound.

The island is quieter these days: a place of seabirds and bays and expertly run farms. There's a stomach-churning gloup, south of Odin Bay, called Vat of Kirbuster, a chambered mound at Ward of Housebay, and a well, south of Whitehall village, the waters of which (if taken in conjunction with the edible seaweed, dulse), tradition claims, will cure every ailment and disease except the Black Death.

Legends abound, too. Like the one surrounding the Mermaids Chair on the crag between Point of Crumey and Point of Lenay at Mill Bay. Scotta Bess, they say, had power over the elements, and would take to sitting in the Mermaids Chair where she would mutter her incantations. Greatly feared, she was seized by a posse of local lads, beaten to death with flails (which, at no comfort to her, had first been washed in Holy Water), then buried deeply in a nearby field. Shocked to see her body lying on the surface of the field the following morning, they then dumped the poor women's corpse into the loch known as Meikle Water, then, all through the night from a relay of boats, piled turfs from the loch shore on top of the not-to-be-put-down witch. And so it was that Meikle Water's wee island was formed, on which, it is told, a swan nests each year.

The tiny island of Papa Stronsay (Papa: priest isle) to the north-east, gives shelter to the pier at Stronsay. It also figures in the Sagas. For it was here that Earl Thorfinn killed his cousin and rival ruler, Rognvald Brusason, one dark night in December

1045. Realizing the house was surrounded, Rognvald vaulted over a circle of his foes and vanished into the night; only to be betrayed down at the shore by the barking of his lap-dog. A historical fact which strengthens my long-held belief that those four-legged friends who never let you down, do — gleefully!

It's a short and uneventful final haul to Kirkwall. The hold is empty now. Camcorder Man returns his new toy to its multi-zipped bag, and a Welsh male-voice choir belt out Men of Harlech from the television set, to an audience of one, stretched out and oblivious in the fag-fugged uptop lounge.

WESTRAY

Westray is similar in plan to Sanday, though more pterodactyl, I think, than lobster. It is the largest and most prosperous of the North Isles, and has the best of both worlds topographically: flattish and inhabited to the south-east, and hilly along the peaty north-west fringes. Although beef cattle farming is the mainstay of the island's economy, there's also a shellfish processing plant, a society of knitters, an hotel, boarding house, self-catering cottages and caravans, and a maker of straw-back Orkney chairs. We called them strae-back chairs, when they were a common, battered and much-used item of rural furniture; not the signed and numbered craftworks they are now; splendidly made though they be.

Birdwatchers will make a birdline for Noup Head cliffs to the north-west, which is a Site of Special Scientific Interest, and reserve of the Royal Society for the Protection of Birds (phew!) The entire island, come to that, is a haven for birds rare and common. There are rich pastures (not pickings!) for the plant enthusiast, on cliff-top and inland heath: sea pink, alphine bistort, meadow rue, primrose.

Haunters — like me — of places and things archaeological wont be disappointed either. Noltland Castle to the west of Bay of Pierowall, will come as something of a surprise to the unprepared traveller. Though roofless and never completed, it is a most impressive and highly sophisticated example of a sixteenth century castle, with many gun-loops, square towers, kitchen, storeroom, a massive fireplace, and a spacious stairway (one of the finest of its kind in Scotland), leading from the entrance, to the great hall. There's a school of thought which claims it was built originally by Bishop Thomas Tulloch sometime in the fifteenth century, though its recorded historical presence resurfaces in the sixteenth century when the castle became the property of one, Gilbert Balfour, court hanger-on and peripatetic opportunist associated with the court of Mary, Queen of Scots. Balfour was involved in the murder of Cardinal Beaton of St Andrews, and Mary, Queen of Scots' consort, Lord Darnley. The castle was later seized by Mary's half-brother, Robert Stewart, and Balfour hot-footed it to Scandinavia where he went into the service of the King of Sweden. Bad blood will out, though, for he became involved in a plot to kill his employer, and was hanged for treason in 1576.

The now ruined Lady Kirk on the Bay of Pierowall, was built in the late seventeeth century. Traces of the original thirteenth century building can be seen in the south wall.

Westray — or Vestrey, as the Norsemen called it — figures throughout the Orkneyinga Saga, and in 1983 the remains of a large Norse settlement was found near the ruins of Westside Church, not far from Ness of Tucquoy. Viking graves were unearthed, too, in the vicinity of the harbour at Pierowall: that well-bielded refuge from human predator and storm.

Legend has it that the so-called Gentlemen's Cave on the rocky coastline west of Noltland Castle, provided a complete winters bolt hole from the clutches of government spies, to a Balfour of Trenabie and his Jacobite mates, whose sym-pathisers, for years to come, continued to drink the dubious health of their blousy and would-be 'king over the water'. (They weren't spawned from that grandly pragmatic and refreshingly cynical Orcadian stock I know and love so well, that's for sure) The cave, the Orkney Tourist Board tell me, though seemingly inaccessible from the land, can still be visited under the guidance of a responsible and knowledgeable local. Happy landings . . .

There are other sites and sights too numerous to mention. I could, but I won't spoil the joy of personal discovery, which no amount of pamphlets — or books for that matter — could ever hope to rival.

PAPA WESTRAY

Small really *is* beautiful and comes packaged four miles long by one mile wide, on the island of Papa Westray — or Papey in meiri, the Greater Priest-island, as it was known in the Sagas.

It was to this holy isle that the slain body of the much-loved Earl Rognvald Brusason was brought for burial in 1046; though where exactly, no one knows.

On the fringes of the Loch of Tredwell (Triduana) in the south of the island, is the site and scant remains of an ancient chapel dedicated to Triduana who, according to legend, was one of two abbesses who accompanied St Boniface (Roman Catholic suppressor of Irish or columban Christianity, who was killed by heathens near Leeuwarden) to the land of the Picts, where, it is claimed, the Pictish king, Nechtan, fell for her. She fled, but was pursued by Nechtan's messenger to tell her now the sight of her gorgeous eyes had caused him to act in such an unkingly fashion. Upon which, she gouged out her eyes, skewered them kabab-like on a twig, and told the messenger to present his master with those very objects he so much admired.

She retired to Restalrig, Midlothian, and devoted the rest of her life to fasting and prayer. The fifteenth century St Triduana's Chapel adjoining Restalrig Parish Church, Restalrig Road South, in Edinburgh, is dedicated to her memory.

There's a fine Norse, hog-backed gravestone in the shape of a Viking house, in the burial ground of St Boniface's Church to the north-west of Loch of Tredwell. An early Christian cross-slab found here, can be seen in Tankerness House Museum, Kirkwall.

On legends: it wasn't that long ago that a famous Papa Westray witch-doctor who, on nursing the sick, would first ask whether an enemy or close friend of her patient had died recently. If the answer was in the affirmative, she would take earth from that person's grave and prescribe a spoonful of the stuff to be mixed with the patient's meals. Mind you, I've had worse in my young days. Gregory's mixture, for one! The thought of which, even now as I write, causes my palms to sweat.

Then there was that well-known Orcadian cure-all for a bleeding nose, where the nostrils were plugged with reeking-fresh pigs dung. And a cupful of sweetened urine, would you believe, did wonders for sufferers of jaundice. And milk in which ...

Papa Westray's northern snout at Mull Head, like that of big brother, Westray, is a nature reserve, RSPB bird sanctuary, and home to the largest Arctic tern colony in north-west Europe. It was here, too, that the last great auk was shot in 1813, and now gazes glassily across some room in London's Natural History Museum.

Again, like Westray, the soil here is fertile and rich. A fact which must have induced the Ancient Ones to settle. Knap of Howar is a well preserved Neolithic farmstead which lies on the south-west edge of the shore of that name. Excavated from a twelve-foot-deep covering of drifted sand during the early nineteen-thirties, it is an interesting — some say unique — example of a small, one-family farmstead, with a dwelling house (its doorway, jambs and checks still intact), and an adjacent and multi-purpose workshop-cum-barn. Tools of bone and stone, plus fragments of decorated domestic pottery, and other household artifacts, were discovered at this, the oldest standing house in Western Europe.

Nearby Holland House with its crow-stepped farm buildings, formerly the home of the Traills of Holland, is worth looking at, if only to underline how inappropriate and shabby most of Scotlands modern housing has become.

There are three chambered cairns on the Holm of Papa, off the east coast of Papa Westray; the southernmost of which is the largest. Like Maes Howe, there are side cells opening off a main rectangular chamber. The difference being, that this one measures some fifty, to sixty feet in length. Some chamber! For Good measure, there are fascinating decorative circles, zig-zags, and socalled 'eyebrow' motifs carved on the walls by those involved in the building and subsequent management of the tomb.

Meanwhile, back in Papa Westray: there's a self-catering hostel, which is light years away from those grim, penitential blocks of my youth; friendly bed and breakfast accommodation in some of the farms; a healthy community co-operative, primary school, craft workshops. And what's more, the one and a half mile flight from Westray to Papa Westray's airfield takes two minutes, and is listed in the Guinness Book of Records as the world's shortest scheduled air flight.

NORTH RONALDSAY

'Hey ... I mean ... just look at that!' he said, pointing outwards and downwards from his starboard window-seat. 'And there's houses on it too! So vulnerable. Flat. Like the sea's patiently waiting to drown the lot.'

My southern colleague had summed-up the collective reactions of us all, as our small, chartered plane flew over the green, silver-fringed island of North Ronaldsay.

This most northerly, and on some ways most feudal of Orkney's North Isles, is also the most unique. A mere three and a half miles long, by two miles wide at its broadest, southernmost end, it is extremely well cultivated. The entire perimeter is bound by a six foot high drystane dyke, built to keep sheep *out*. For these are multi-hued seaweed nibbling creatures, who chomp their way contentedly along the foreshore, on strips of land called *the ness*. The yowes are brought inside the dyke at lambing time, to feed on succulent grass; then returned to the shore with their knock-kneed bairns. The seasons of clipping and dipping are shared ones, as they still are in a few farms soothaboot.

It's not surprising, given the flat, and, on days of mist, the near invisibility of the island, that many ships have been wrecked on the skerries. Sixteen vessels foundered in the space of fifteen years before the first lighthouse was erected in 1789 on Dennis Head. The stone-built, ball-capped tower of the original lighthouse is worth the wee daunder, from the road at Bewan, next to Dennis Loch. The keeper's house is a sad, crow-stepped ruin. The present white-banded lighthouse was lit in 1854, and is the highest land-rooted beacon in Britain, and a godsend for those who ply the North Atlantic seas.

Given the islands remoteness, it is no surprise to learn that not only the ancient dialect, but many of the old customs survived here, longer than on Mainland the South Isles. The Statistical Account of 1794 records one in which a New Years Day gathering of fifty locals would sing and dance in the moonlight, round the standing stone at nearby Loch Gretchen.

Although there are no ancient monuments comparable to some I've mentioned, the excavation in the late nineteenth century of the Broch of Burrian on the shore of Strom Ness, revealed some splendid Pictish and Early Christian objects: a stone incised with a Celtic cross, an iron Sanctus bell, and a fragment of ox bone, carved on one side with a disc with notched rectangle, and a crescent and v-rod, on the other.

Like its northerly neighbour, Fair Isle, North Ronaldsay is a temporary resting place for itinerant birds. Wild flowers — to coin a phrase — grow in great profusion. Seen-it-all-before seals loll about the rocks and beaches. And the air smells like a newly-opened oyster.

EPILOGUE
A Chance Find

Shortly after my father's death, I was sifting through the contents of a chest of drawers, when I discovered a penny jotter tucked away behind caringly stacked winter woolies and laundered shirts. The dozen or so pages, penned in his neat italic hand, were headed 'Memories of a Boy From Sooth Aboot.' Scanning the pages, it was obvious that I'd chanced upon private gleanings from his very first visit to Orkney in 1910; three years after the premature death of his father, who had left Orkney to further his short-lived career as a telephone engineer in Inverness.

I can think of no fitting way, then, other than to conclude my own celebration of islands with a few paragraphs from his recollections of that idyllic summer's month, eighty-two years ago.

'I was ten years old. My knowledge of Orkney was very limited, but the little I had heard from my father, plus my own romantic notions, had built up a picture of a place so different to any I had known in southern parts.

My uncle met me at the foot of the gangway. His smile was open, his welcome warm. His speech — what I could understand of it — seemed to me to have decided biblical characteristics with his use of the words 'thee' and 'thu'. He was a big man. He heaved me and my bag into a horse-drawn farm cart at the head of the pier, and I cannot imagine that the bairns of Kirkwall would have let that rare sight pass without comment. The city boy fae soothaboot in his school uniform: an Eton collar, stiff boots, and a blue Balmoral with toorie and fluttering ribbon.

His house tallied with my expectations. The roof was thatched, and a peat fire burned in the hearth; above which hung a huge three-toed black pot. There was cool buttermilk to be had for the taking; pork hanging from the rafters; a fussing aunt, and a horse to ride bareback in the yard.

The tiny country church, too, intrigued me. It was lit by oil lamps. The minister gave out the number of the first Psalm, but no organ notes filled the church. A man stood up, struck a tuning fork on a table and, with a few preliminary 'Doh, Doh, Dohs, and Mee, Mee, Mees,' launched the singing. This same man a few years later, made me my first suit of long trousers, and a very fine suit it was.

On the last day of my holiday, my aunt wanted to give me a hen to take home to my mother. She was ill and in bed, and none of my cousins would volunteer to kill the bird. I said I would, if she could tell me how. So I stood at her bedside with the live hen, followed her instructions, and wrung the poor thing's neck. Priding myself on a job well done, I laid it on the floor, when, to my surprise, it opened one eye, got onto its feet and strutted out of the door. The sad craitur had its head near torn from its neck before I finally managed to kill it. My uncle bellowed with laughter when he heard the tale.

I had come to Orkney with a great degree of anticipation. I left with a huge sadness. After weeks of happy and care-free living, I now had to return to the school where I was boarded, with its regimentation, cold baths, and harsh discipline.

As the ship pulled away from the quay, I remember turning my back to the passengers, to hide my tears.'

Further Reading

Baily, Patrick. *Orkney* (David and Charles. 1985)

Brown, George Mackay, and Werner Forman. *Portrait of Orkney.* (The Hogarth Press. London. 1981)

Firth, John. *Reminiscences of an Orkney Parish* (Stromness. Printed by W. R. Rendall. 1974)

Gunn, J. *Orkney the Magnetic North.* (Thomas Nelson and Sons Ltd. 1941)

Hedges, John W. *Tomb of the Eagles.* (John Murray. 1987)

Marwick, Hugh. *The County Books: Orkney.* (Robert Hale Ltd. 1951)

Marwick, Ernest W. *The Folklore of Orkney and Shetland.* (B. T. Batsford Ltd. London. 1975)

Ritchie, Anna. *Exploring Scotlands Heritage: Orkney and Shetland.* (The Royal Commission on the Ancient and Historical Monuments of Scotland, 1985)

Schei, Liv Kjörsvik, and Gunnie Moberg *The Orkney Story.* (B. T. Batsford Ltd. London. 1985)

Saga, Orkneyinga. (Translated by Hermann Polsson and Paul Edwards. Penguin Classics. Penguin Books. 1982)

Index

89